THE VISONE METHOD

THE VISONE METHOD

A New Philosophy in
Early Childhood Education

Carmine and Phyllis Visone
with Doreen Nagle,
author of ***Parenting in a Nutshell***

iUniverse Star
New York   Bloomington

THE VISONE METHOD
A New Philosophy in Early Childhood Education

iUniverse Star
an iUniverse, Inc. imprint

iUniverse books may be ordered through booksellers or by contacting:

iUniverse
1663 Liberty Drive
Bloomington, IN 47403
www.iuniverse.com
1-800-Authors (1-800-288-4677)

Because of the dynamic nature of the Internet, any Web addresses or links contained in this book may have changed since publication and may no longer be valid.

The views expressed in this work are solely those of the author and do not necessarily reflect the views of the publisher, and the publisher hereby disclaims any responsibility for them.

Photographs by Al Dazio

ISBN: 978-1-935278-51-1(pbk)
ISBN: 978-1-935278-52-8 (ebk)

Library of Congress Control Number: 2009925378

Printed in the United States of America

To Our Children

Keith Michael
Jaime Lynn
Kristen Mary

We hold their hands for a short time, but they touch our hearts ... forever.

—Phyllis and Carmine Visone

Contents

PART I
THE VISONE METHOD

Chapter 1

Chapter 2

Chapter 3

PART IV
THE VISONE METHOD IN ACTION:
PRESCHOOL THROUGH SECOND GRADE

PART V
PULLING IT ALL TOGETHER

Foreword

Home Away From Home Academy (HAFHA) is a beacon of hope for contemporary early childhood education. The founders of this academy, Phyllis and Carmine Visone, have developed an instructional model that will certainly influence the millennial curriculum and will no doubt be widely replicated.

One only needs to make a short visit to the Aberdeen, New Jersey, campus to realize that it is an extraordinary place to grow and learn. As you approach the entrance, you feel the positive, welcoming energy of the school. You're immediately taken in by the beautiful faces of a multicultural population and awed by vibrant children's creations that make up the delightful landscape of the school.

Rigorous and simultaneously joyful classrooms resonate with the sounds of laughter, music, movement, and total engagement of the people within. Teachers, children, and parents genuinely like and trust one another. They listen, talk, and respond to each other, creating a harmonious, supportive social tone that fosters self-realization and societal well-being.

This school's remarkable story started in 1993. Phyllis and Carmine's vision was to start small in order to develop a core culture and philosophical base that would challenge the status quo and enable the HAFHA community of learners to make valid decisions about their future programs, procedures, processes, and methodologies.

Their comprehensive approach to planning using quality, research-based principles focuses on students' diverse needs and ensures mastery of a world-class curriculum. The application of Howard Gardner's theory of multiple intelligences drives the instructional model, stimulating students to develop a broader spectrum of their potential by using their abilities to explore, discover, analyze, and view outcomes with multiple lenses of the brain.

The success of Home Away From Home Academy is a testimony to the unique and effective management of Phyllis and Carmine. As advocates of the arts, they lead with creativity, imagination, humor, and panache. They believe that every day is a celebration of life and learning, and they afford both adults and children abundant opportunities to embrace individual presentations and school-wide extravaganzas across the curriculum.

This book offers a revolutionary early education method that intertwines research-based theory, best educational practices, a dash of common sense, and a positive school environment. I, personally, want to thank the Visones on behalf of the multitude of children who have benefited from their wisdom, energy, expertise, love of the educational process, and most important, love of the little people!

—Irene Sessa

Irene Sessa, an educator for over forty years, pioneered the Universal Pre-Kindergarten Program as a principal on Staten Island. Both a Curriculum and Early Childhood Specialist, Ms. Sessa is currently engaged with New Visions, a nonprofit educational organization, mentoring new principals in the five boroughs of New York City.

Introduction

Children arrive in this world eager to learn. In fact, in the time between birth and six years of age we learn 50 percent of what we need *for our lifetime*. The Visone Method centers on guiding healthy children between the ages of three months through second grade in their own development: investigating their environment, learning to communicate, and, within a relatively short period of time, constructing theories about how things work. Step by step, the Method specifically identifies the most credible procedures for each particular stage and age of development to ensure high-quality early childhood education.

The Visone Method, as fully described in this book, is based on the findings from the programs we have successfully implemented over the past decade in the school we own and operate, Home Away From Home Academy (HAFHA) in Aberdeen, New Jersey. More than 2,500 students have passed through the thresholds of HAFHA in the decade since its opening, each of them benefitting from the philosophies, strategies, and techniques embedded in The Visone Method. These procedures absolutely work! Studies prove that 70 percent of the children who have been through our program remain in the top 10 percent of their class, even after a decade of schooling. Furthermore, a full 30 percent of our students are invited into Gifted and Talented Education (GATE) programs.

It is our belief that this book belongs not only on the bookshelves of every educator, but also in the hands of every parent—because a child's family is his first and most important teacher. The main purpose of this book is to give parents and teachers a complete and new understanding of how a child's learning develops in the early years, so that their children can benefit as the children of HAFHA have. The Visone Method is a *proven* philosophy we strongly recommend to all who influence vulnerable, eager young minds and emotions. While our philosophy is a commonsense approach to early childhood education, what makes it extraordinary is that it considers the whole child at *every* turn.

Our proven success **challenges** the widely held belief that the early childhood years are strictly about fun, a time to fill with meaningless play-without-purpose until children can be enrolled in "real" school. Our results also challenge the belief that whatever a child learns during the early years will soon be forgotten. In fact, our results suggest the exact opposite.

The ages between infancy and six are vitally important years when significant lifelong learning takes place. What your young child learns today will stick with him or her for a lifetime. Why not make it the best?

We have enthusiasm and love for what we teach, and we are confident that the children you care for will greatly benefit from The Visone Method. Welcome to a new era in childhood education!

—Phyllis and Carmine Visone

PART I
THE VISONE METHOD

Chapter 1
The Visone Method's Philosophies

The Visone Method is proof that a brainstorm can become a masterpiece. As all methods do, The Visone Method began with philosophy—basic conjecture that we had to examine, test, and finally prove. In this chapter, we'll take a look at the philosophies that inspired and are now the foundation for The Visone Method and discuss how they are implemented at HAFHA.

Children Need a Loving, Comforting, Safe, and Clean Environment

Walk the halls of HAFHA and you will repeatedly hear and see the first philosophy of The Visone Method: children are learning in an environment where they feel safe, loved, comforted, and comfortable.

> "When my son was afraid of the fire alarm sound, you called off the drill for the day. It made us both feel like we were protected and that we both mattered. Then you told me that you would take his hand before you rang the alarm the next time. Knowing that you were so sensitive to his fear has calmed my nerves." —*Linda Novotny, parent*

Realizing that young children learn best when they are totally at ease in their surroundings, as well as in the care of the adults with whom they spend their day, we made policies that would ensure such an environment at every turn. It's not enough to have a thorough knowledge of procedures and curriculum alone; teachers—indeed, all staff members—must handle situations in a calm, kind-hearted manner, using intuitiveness, flexibility, and open-mindedness.

The Visone Method teachers genuinely care about and love working with children; these are not qualities that can be faked. A teacher's temperament and personality are extremely important components of The Visone Method: HAFHA fills classrooms solely with teachers who are patient and use humor; they have a sincere respect for the little learners in their care. Teachers who are positive in their approach help mold children into happy, curious students who feel safe and cocooned. When children feel safe, they become less anxious, more outgoing, and more confident in themselves. This is the basis for self-esteem.

The Visone Method ensures that a teacher would never make a child feel embarrassed about anything he might say, think, or do. In addition, teachers follow discipline strategies that enhance the child's learning experience and increase self-esteem. For instance, a disruptive child is escorted from the area, and a conversation follows that includes statements about what he did ("You hit Johnny"), why that was not okay ("It hurt Johnny's feelings"), and how it can be amended ("When you are ready, we can go back and you can tell Johnny that you are sorry"). Discipline, then, becomes a teaching opportunity.

A loving teacher warmly welcoming children as they walk into the classroom is critically important, especially during those first tenuous days of being separated from home, thrust into a strange new environment without moms or dads for assurance. The way in which children are initiated into a new environment, such as an early childhood facility, is instrumental in developing their ability to trust people who enter their lives as they grow into their adult years.

The safety of each child is as important to The Visone Method's educators as it is to the parents who send their children to our school. This commitment to safety includes ensuring the cleanliness of the building in which the child spends her day, as well as teaching her about personal hygiene.

> "Your child is entitled to the right to a clean, safe classroom equipped with carefully selected equipment designed to foster the development of the whole child."—*Welcome to Home Away From Home Academy* pamphlet

Whether it's spelled out in the Health Policy Manual or pinned in a prominent place in each classroom, this very important dictum is followed by HAFHA employees at every turn: maintaining a safe, healthy, and clean environment is fundamental to supporting a great learning environment.

Not only does HAFHA keep a nurse on staff, but teachers in the infant rooms are trained emergency medical technicians (EMTs), as well. All teachers, including the director, are also trained in CPR.

Cleaning solutions, kept under lock and key, are used following a prescribed procedure to keep areas in tip-top, germ-free order. Tables and toys are first washed with soap and water, followed by a bath in diluted bleach solution. Sheets on cots are washed weekly, more frequently if needed. All teachers receive training about the proper, sanitary way to change diapers.

Socket covers, padded corners, and round-edged furniture are all carefully selected and used. The smoke detectors in every room, the fire extinguishers, and the fire alarm system are all inspected regularly.

In addition, staff members rigidly follow the safety procedure of releasing children only to the people who have permission to take them home.

Every Child Is a Unique Individual with Value and Rights

Children, as surely as adults, are individuals. Individuals learn at their own pace and in their own way. The Visone Method, based on a behaviorist philosophy that builds self-esteem, recognizes that children have distinct learning styles (auditory, kinesthetic, visual, or tactile), interests, and areas in which they excel or need more attention.

For example, most very young children have not yet developed the ability to express themselves in words, yet they still need teachers who can tend to their feelings. A teacher who can say, "I see that you are upset because you didn't get to play with the train first. Maybe we can find another train to play with," not only makes the child feel like an individual, but also helps her understand her own feelings, putting her squarely on the road to developing a sense of self.

A teacher who allows a child to explore building blocks on her own fosters self-esteem when she acknowledges the child's efforts: "You are a very good builder." A teacher who then asks about what the student has built in an open-ended way ("Can you tell me about what you built?"), as opposed to making a judgment on the project ("Is that supposed to be a bridge?"), recognizes a child's blossoming uniqueness.

This recognition of uniqueness extends to the child's cultural and religious heritage as well: the school must treat all faiths and customs with equal respect.

We are so strongly committed to each individual student who comes through the HAFHA doors that we print a "Statement of Commitments to Your Child" in the welcoming pamphlet given to parents. It says, in part, that each child:

- Is valued for his or her unique personality and contribution to the group
- Has the right to a variety of developmentally enriching educational opportunities in an atmosphere of loving care
- Has the right to the attention inherent in the name of the school, Home Away From Home

We are personally committed to teaching styles and policies that promote these beliefs, incorporating individuality, fostering self-confidence, and nurturing a positive self-image for each child.

A First Experience Will Be Carried by the Child for a Lifetime

Attending an early childhood education facility is often a child's first experience of being away from home. Teachers carry an immense responsibility that is a natural part of the job: they employ positive approaches that the child can build upon over his lifetime.

The Visone Method realizes that small children's hearts and minds are very fragile; therefore, teachers who take on the job of educating young children must be particularly honest in their love of their work. Young, impressionable children—ready to be molded—have built-in radar that lets them know when they are not being dealt with honestly.

We include this statement at the beginning of the "Welcome to Home Away From Home Academy" pamphlet: "By creating a sheltered, nurturing environment in which each child is made to feel safe, secure, and emotionally comfortable, the staff promotes a foundation for intellectual growth, social skills and, ultimately, academic excellence that the majority of students carry forward throughout their school years."

Since a first experience will be carried by the child for a lifetime, it is our belief that teachers must, without exception, dedicate all their energies to the class, instilling in each child a lust for learning, new experiences, and exploration. It is so important, in fact, that one of the evaluation criteria for teachers at HAFHA is how well they use positive motivation.

Children Learn Through Play

One of the most important ways to give children that lust for learning is through play. Play is a child's job. It prepares them for the world in which they will grow up. Just as you might work at your job each day, children have their daily job: play! A quality early childhood education program, as prescribed by The Visone Method, is not a babysitting service: it's a place for children to develop socially, academically, cognitively, emotionally, and physically.

There are two approaches, both important, in teaching through play: one is free play with purpose, and the other is play in structured settings mindfully developed to teach through fun. Both approaches have the same goal: to advance the child's physical, intellectual, and emotional competencies. Also known as the developmental approach, this method incorporates play activities into the curriculum. Children taught under The Visone Method learn a lot, but they always have fun.

A fundraiser for the community turns into a Hop-A-Thon, which subsequently builds gross motor skills. Reporting the day's weather to classmates at Circle Time is a lesson in science and public speaking that also builds self-confidence. Creating with paints and paintbrushes helps children develop brain synapses, while increasing fine motor skills and encouraging exploration of their creative abilities. Yet these "lessons" are also play.

Children arrive in the world with an innate quest to explore what's around them. They are often referred to as "little sponges," passionately soaking up early experiences. When fun is introduced into lessons—as opposed to the old approach of teaching by repetition and memorization—children remember and internalize the lessons. Learning becomes natural and easy. The Visone Method says, "Once children are less anxious, they become more outgoing, gain more confidence, and learn to love themselves. Then, you can teach them anything."

The Visone Method takes advantage of teaching through play by offering such heady curriculum as science and language early—always with a fun bent. Take HAFHA's annual Science Fair, for example, which has grown so popular it takes place in the ballroom of a local hall.

At the Fair, six-year-olds have won ribbons for describing "How the Human Eye Works." In one case, a student, only five at the time, had the idea to become the science project himself; in "The Human Eye and Amblyopia" (commonly referred to as "lazy eye"), he demonstrated how an eye patch improved his own eye condition. Another budding scientist tried to answer the question: Which cleans better, bleach or detergent? By taking equally dirtied T-shirts covered with splotches of mustard, oil, berries, and soy sauce, this future Madame Curie won second prize for her observations.

Other Science Fair projects range from weather experiments, digestion, and electricity to answering that age-old question: "Why is the sky blue?" Themes are limited only by the student's imagination. Little hands work to put together projects and experiments from simple things found around the house—like flashlights, detergent, and snack foods—as well as items found outside the house—water, sand, and plants. Through their experiments, the children learn principles of science firsthand. Since they've had fun doing it, the lesson is retained.

To encourage all students in their pursuit of scientific principles, as well as to give each a self-esteem boost, HAFHA sends every scientist home with a Certificate of Recognition to proudly show off to their families. Once HAFHA parents see the results of the methods we use to instill a love of learning, they are often inspired to make comments, as this mother did: "My daughter absolutely loves science now … HAFHA's fun approach (is responsible)."

Back in the classroom, little HAFHA scientists continue having fun by learning to make "play clay" from ingredients found around the house, observing as the mixture changes from individual ingredients to something recognizable. Then they turn the clay into one-of-a-kind art pieces. At HAFHA, students as young as preschool-age are introduced to science using simple observation techniques. Going the extra step, we employ a teacher who specializes in science to come into the preschool classrooms twice every month and weekly for kindergarten through second grades.

Math, language, science, and other lessons are taught in classroom areas filled with games that allow the children to learn letters of the alphabet, days of the week, matching, sorting, and much more. Butterflies, magnets, and rocks are available to be explored. Writing centers, where children are free to express themselves, are stocked with everything a beginning writer needs. Reading centers house a wide variety of books for both beginning and more advanced readers.

Easily accessible glue, glitter, paper, paints, and brushes in varying sizes offer opportunities to exercise fine motor skills, and children can discuss hues and shades, as well as experiment in creating those colors. Children are encouraged to use their critical thinking skills and imaginations—as well as prepare for the grownup world—by dressing up in costumes from the classroom costume box, playing with child-sized kitchen "appliances," or testing new skills on musical instruments.

We are firm believers in music as a superb teaching tool: it is a known fact that young children learn better when song and rhythm are utilized instead of speech alone. Our teaching staff is seen—and heard—putting this philosophy to work every day; they frequently sing with the children. In addition, music is played in the background while the children work on their various projects; the little students are encouraged to sing along when appropriate.

Each day in each classroom, time for songs and music is built into the schedule. Finger movements act out songs; rhythm instruments are played; individual instrumental sounds are learned; directions via song are followed. There are songs for cleaning up, to greet the morning, or say goodbye for the day—music is fun with a purpose.

At HAFHA, we take it even deeper: Pre-kindergarten through second-grade HAFHA students perform in an annual musical production, such as *The Music Man*, *Bye Bye Birdie*, *The Wizard of Oz*, or *Grease*. Costumes, sets, cordless microphones, dialogue, singing, and dancing—nothing and no one is left out. This extraordinary event is fully staged Broadway-style and performed live in front of a packed audience. The production's aim is to include as many of the students as possible onstage in each scene and number. The community response is so warm that, again, an outside facility is rented to accommodate every playgoer.

Preschoolers perform their own musical, but on a slightly less extravagant and more age-appropriate scale. The results: happy, eager young actors who have shared the experience of a lifetime, which has enhanced their self-confidence and fired their imaginations. They have also learned many subtle social and emotional lessons as a result of their experience.

Music is an international language. It can break barriers and change moods even as it teaches language, grows pathways in a child's brain, and leads to better math scores. A teacher does not have to have a great singing voice to qualify under The Visone Method, but must have a love for singing and playing music with students.

Playtime with poetry is another experience to which HAFHA students are exposed. One poetry event occurs at a local national chain bookstore. Excited students clamor into the store's children's section as they stand, one by one, to recite either a favorite poem or one they have composed on their own, perhaps a result of a classroom lesson. In addition to writing and/or memorizing their piece of poetry, students learn other valuable lessons as they prepare, such as reading with intonation or waiting patiently for their turn.

Foreign language, another prominent subject on the HAFHA curriculum roster, is taught in a fun way. It is a proven fact that children have the ability to learn a second language at a very young age. Too many schools do not recognize this fact and teach a second language only to children much older than HAFHA's students, making it more difficult for those children to speak the new language like a native.

At HAFHA, teachers who specialize in Italian, French, and Spanish bring their expertise directly into the class, starting in preschool. While there is a tremendous advantage in being bilingual in today's multicultural society, children who learn a foreign language during an early period of brain development also learn to respect different cultures and heritages.

Infants and toddlers, who too often are viewed as not "doing anything" yet, are also given many opportunities to develop and have fun using The Visone Method. HAFHA is fully equipped with soft pillows and mats for climbing on, toys that promote stretching, grabbing, and rolling, ride-on toys, parachutes to hide under, and fabric tunnels to crawl through.

In addition to lessons designed to promote physical and academic development, every HAFHA student enjoys plenty of free time to explore the ever-evolving, enriched resources and materials, including games, books, music, furnishings, toys, balls, paints, crafts, and much, much more, available to them in open, spacious, bright, cheerful, and stimulating classrooms. Outside, bikes and seesaws join a host of toys and play equipment. When a child can select toys safely, he can start to make important choices and form personal likes and dislikes.

By weaving fun and play into its curriculum, The Visone Method ensures that its young students will retain what they learn and have a jump on their peers within every area of early education.

The Right Teachers Are Imperative for Success

"Your child is entitled to the best in early childhood education from a professional, nurturing teaching staff."
—*Welcome to Home Away From Home Academy pamphlet*

HAFHA is unique in many superb ways, but in the requirements it demands of its teachers, it excels. All teachers must be certified and must have, at minimum, an associate's degree. Some teachers on the HAFHA payroll have their master's degrees, and some have more than twenty years' teaching experience.

There are several ways a teacher can be considered certified:

1. A four-year degree in early childhood education or a four-year degree in elementary education (preferable for a preschool teacher)

2. A P–3 certification covering preschool through third-grade education

3. An associate's degree in early childhood education

4. A Child Development Associate certification with courses geared to ages zero to five

However, it's not enough to only have a strong, appropriate educational background. Teachers must know how to transform their education appropriately in the classroom. This requirement is an imperative for success. Without the best and most committed teachers in the classroom to carry out The Visone Method of early childhood education, the Method would be an unfulfilled philosophy. The development of the students relies on the success and the quality of the programs taught; but, every day, it is the teacher in the classroom who holds the key.

It takes a true professional to work respectfully with young children, to allow each child his or her own pace, to turn each moment into a teaching moment, while at the same time remaining flexible to fit everyone's needs into the curriculum. We also know it takes a compassionate, knowledgeable teacher to gain the trust of the children in their care. Teachers need to understand each child's family background and incorporate that into the child's experience. They need to be able to advocate for children one minute and get down to play at eye level the next. It takes an intuitive, educated, observant teacher who is a kid at heart and dedicated to her core.

Our teachers follow a code of ethics that allows children their individuality, creativity, and self-respect, while guiding them in social and moral values. A lot is expected from a teacher at HAFHA. They ascribe to these Top 10 Values:

- Educational Excellence

- Professionalism

- Integrity

- Innovation

- Morality

- Teamwork and Communication

- Nurturing

- Equality and Tolerance

- Accountability

- Respect

In addition, they are evaluated on fifty aspects of their abilities, including such basics as how well they arrange artwork and posters at a child's-eye level in the classroom. Do they encourage cultural identity through the use of ethnic displays? Is the room rearranged for variety? How well does the teacher prepare lessons that promote emotional health, creativity, cognitive abilities, physical abilities, and readiness skills?

As responsible adults, we plan for the futures of our children and ourselves. Responsible schools must also plan for the future. Therefore, the HAFHA teaching staff gets many opportunities to attend workshops (many offered on the HAFHA campus) so that they may do the important work of keeping current with cutting-edge methods in early childhood education. While HAFHA retains its old-fashioned values and morals, it recognizes that incorporating current teaching techniques keeps The Visone Method at the forefront.

Parents Are an Integral Part of the School

"Mostly, thank you for being the reinforcement of our teachings at home … And thank you for sharing the goings on at HAFHA in your monthly newsletter … and a special thank you for the wonderful shows and other events (parents can attend)."—*Miriam A. Leto, parent*

The welcoming pamphlet given to all HAFHA parents says: "Children have the right to a school environment that recognizes his parent as the first and most important teacher in his life and actively nurtures that relationship." Keeping in mind that a child's development is solidly based, first and foremost, on the dedication of his parents, a Visone Method school views itself as being in partnership with the child's family.

Prior to the beginning of each new school year, a parent orientation evening is held, during which school policies are outlined and questions are answered. The *Parent's Handbook* is filled with the details parents need to acclimate themselves, including ways parents can be involved. For instance, parent mailboxes are set up in each classroom for notices to be distributed. The mailbox, which is checked daily, also allows for parent-to-parent communication to set up play dates, etc.

Children are not the only ones who feel at home at Home Away From Home Academy. Parents love the "open door" policy, and they are welcome to visit the school any time. Special events encourage family participation, such as Grandparent's Day, birthday parties, parades, field trips, "dates" with parents, and special breakfasts. One full week is set aside each November so that parents may observe their children while the class is in progress. All parents are encouraged to share any special talents and experiences with their child's class.

Infants and toddlers go home with a daily report detailing his or her day. A "What we did today" report is posted for parents of all preschoolers; information on what topics were covered, stories read, or songs sung helps parents start a conversation with their little ones about their days. This is invaluable to parent-child communication, because young children who get into the habit of talking with their parents tend to keep that up as they enter the more reticent teen years. (What parent wouldn't like to have their teen tell them about their day?)

At pick-up time, HAFHA teachers take the time to remember something special a child did or a new milestone achieved to share with the parent. Questions or comments that parents may have during the school day are given prompt attention. Because we are onsite, the turnaround time in getting a private meeting with us is minimal, if not immediate.

One of our goals is to keep parents informed about positive parenting techniques. To that end, we keep a variety of informative parenting articles and books at the ready to pass along. Parents are warmly welcome to discuss concerns with any of the teachers in a private setting.

As part of our commitment to ongoing assessments of each child's development, we stress the importance of parent-teacher conferences. Held twice each school year, conferences are an opportunity for parents and teachers to work together to identify goals that have been met and ones that need to be worked toward and to determine what role parents and teachers should take in helping the child to achieve these goals.

One of the most popular ways we keep families involved is through a jam-packed monthly newsletter. Articles about science experiments, news from each classroom, a column from the school nurse, tips on how to dress a child for school, lots of photos of HAFHA's kids in action, fun rhymes, parenting advice—it's all in there. The average HAFHA newsletter is twenty-eight pages full, as opposed to the standard two-sided sheet produced by most schools—if at all!

A School Should Connect with the Community

"I wanted to extend the thanks of all of us at St. Vincent's Hospital for the beautiful expressions of support in response to the World Trade Center disaster. Your cards were a much-needed message of hope here at the hospital. We are grateful to have you as members of our team."
—*Jane Connorton, president*

"We would like to thank all the wonderful people that gave so generously to help us make a difference in the lives of the children that we have helped this holiday season. May God bless the families and staff of Home Away From Home Academy this New Year with good health and much happiness."—*Peggy Karaban*

Ever vigilant for teaching moments that meet several purposes, The Visone Method matches lessons in caring about others with family activities and creative events. Known throughout our community for charity work, we believe that involving students in community concerns exposes children to unselfish acts of giving and kindness. Young children must be taught about compassion; while they may be the center of the universe at home, children must learn to care for and be considerate of others, in order to become well-rounded citizens.

By introducing children to charity work, such as the work HAFHA does on behalf of the Muscular Dystrophy Association, the care packages sent to homesick soldiers, reaching out to 9/11 families, and giving toys to less fortunate children, little ones begin to understand that they are part of a bigger picture. Their eyes widen as the reality of what they are doing sinks in: helping others makes them feel good about themselves. Giving to others underscores just how fortunate they are.

As they pack toys to be shipped, draw handmade cards, hop on one leg for a fundraiser, or contribute money taken from their piggy banks at home to a charity, these children come away with a lesson designed to last a lifetime—giving really *is* better than receiving. We started participating in charities for a reason close to our hearts: we feel so blessed and want to give back.

Our philosophies are put into action every day at HAFHA. You can see evidence of these philosophies in every detail of our physical environment, discipline strategies, teaching techniques, special programs, and communication forums. The parents, children, and staff at HAFHA are aligned in our beliefs about what an early childhood educational facility should promote, promise, and provide—and that's just the beginning of what makes The Visone Method so effective.

Chapter 2
The Visone Method—Nuts and Bolts

Over time, as we honed our philosophies, we simultaneously developed the "nuts and bolts" of The Visone Method. As The Visone Method grew from a philosophy into a concrete, reliable system, we participated in research that strongly confirmed our beliefs. Over 1,000 students were studied after they left kindergarten at HAFHA: 75 percent continued in the top 10 percent of their class throughout elementary school. Our goal—to provide a school where children can have fun, learn, excel, and feel how much they are treasured—has been fulfilled and surpassed.

The Visone Method is a blueprint for every parent of young children and every educator who is given the honor of working with young children.

Our Mission and Vision

Our mission is to create unique educational environments built on sound research and qualified instruction that foster academic excellence. We further believe in instilling an active love of learning by providing experiences that enable all students to acquire a strong foundation during early childhood education.

Our vision is to provide the highest educational alternatives for all students in an expanding, multicultural learning environment supported by enthusiastic educators, innovative programming, and state-of-the-art technology.

The Main Tenets of The Visone Method

- The Visone Method incorporates traditional teaching methods of readiness activities in preparation for entering public school.
- The Visone Method incorporates the behaviorist philosophy of education that builds self-esteem and confidence in children.

18

- The Visone Method incorporates the developmental approach to teaching, encompassing a play curriculum in all activities.

- The Visone Method integrates the groundbreaking philosophies of early childhood education from Montessori, Froebel, and Piaget and defines stages of development.

- The Visone Method incorporates teaching strategies based on the firm belief that learning through play, music, and movement is an extremely successful philosophy of early education.

- The Visone Method plans for young children's social, emotional, physical, and intellectual growth while considering each child as an individual, with his or her own capabilities and rate of development.

- The Visone Method believes in offering a stimulating environment wrapped in loving acceptance.

- The Visone Method not only educates children, but gifts them with a confidence in, and respect for, their own abilities.

- The Visone Method promotes working cooperatively with peers so that children can build on this foundation.

Primary Goals of The Visone Method

- One of the primary goals of The Visone Method is to advance and enhance the development of positive self-esteem in each student, while paving the road for their future education.

- In line with other leaders of early childhood education, as well as committed organizations such as the Association for Childhood Education International, The Visone Method is dedicated to defining the developmental level and learning style of each child, while designing activities to foster the growth of social, intellectual, physical, and emotional skills.

Secondary Goals of The Visone Method

Social and Emotional Development

- To assist the child in developing an understanding of self
- To help the child discover and express feelings in socially acceptable ways
- To establish cooperative behavior
- To provide outlets for encouraging creative growth and individual expression
- To encourage a feeling of cultural identity and acceptance of cultural diversity

Intellectual Development

- To explore and comprehend math concepts, such as classification, sequence, quantities, numeral recognition, and spatial relationships
- To develop proficiency in written and verbal language skills, such as figure-ground relationships, letter recognition, left-to-right progression, initial consonant sounds, and the relationship between spoken and written words
- To examine properties of objects and understand how those properties can be changed
- To be able to process and respond to auditory information
- To promote the development of higher-level thinking skills
- To introduce and enhance technical skills

Physical Development

- To develop fine motor skills, coordination, and dexterity
- To promote the development of gross motor skills
- To develop hand-eye coordination

Our vision, mission, tenets, and goals are the foundation of The Visone Method. Now let's take a look at the curriculum and why we do what we do.

Chapter 3
The Visone Method's Curriculum—Why We Do What We Do

Young minds not only can learn much more than generations past believed possible, but will grasp even higher levels of learning when given the proper tools in a loving, fun, nurturing environment. The daily experiences that a child is exposed to make all the difference. A child who is offered a day filled with stimulating, challenging activities will develop brain connections at a much more rapid rate than a child who has been plopped, unattended, in front of the "one-eyed monster" in the living room—the TV!

The Visone Method curriculum reinforces each child's curiosity and ability to learn by integrating multiple high-level programs and exposing young learners to critical skills and lessons that will set them up for success and serve them for their entire life.

Teaching to Every Child

While all children have some learning traits in common, each child has a learning style as unique as his or her own thumbprint. One child must reason things out himself, another has to "see it" demonstrated to understand how it works, one must picture it in his mind, and another needs to act it out in order to "feel" it. In fact, most children learn through more than one method. By integrating visual, auditory, tactile, and kinesthetic teaching methods, all children have the opportunity to develop musical, artistic, verbal, logical, and physical intelligence.

As mentioned earlier, little ones are like sponges. It falls on the teacher's shoulders, then, to make sure that what gets absorbed and hardwired into a child's brain will strengthen and clarify the child's development, not muddy it.

Science, computers, language, and a healthy dose of music, movement, art, imaginative play, and discovery, presented by a caring adult, are the keys to learning success. These are also the cornerstones of The Visone Method's curriculum.

Supporting the Whole Child

Teaching children has to encompass the whole child, on all levels—not only academically, but also emotionally.

One of the ways a Visone Method school supports the whole child is by supporting the child's family during difficult days. Hard times affect children differently than the same difficult times affect adults. For one thing, children don't have the scope of life experience or vocabulary to define their problems (indeed, many adults lack these attributes).

With divorce, illness, death, economic hardships, and sibling problems as a part of everyday living, family members may sometimes need to "borrow" an ear to tell their troubles to. While not expected to be professional mental health counselors, teachers and other staff must be generous with sympathy, empathy, and real-world resources as needed. At HAFHA, we keep an extensive library of books that support families in crisis. We lend these books to our families without question, as a way to help build their support network.

Our families need to know that each family member is cared about and that our empathy includes sensitivity to the child in our care who is suffering during a family's hard times. It is our role to dig down deep and give tender support and love when one of our children is in crisis. In doing so, we remain a constant in the child's life while the child is in turmoil. This solid support frees the child to become stronger and happier as he works his way out of his problems.

When a child in crisis arrives at school for the day, he knows he can seek refuge and sanctuary there. This gentle stability creates an environment that helps the child stay focused on learning. He knows that if he needs to talk—or retreat—his patient, caring teacher is there to help.

When it comes to children in crisis, Visone Method teachers and staff spend countless hours balancing the proper support with classroom activities. When a child is ready to talk about a problem, teachers combine the resources found on our bookshelves with their own empathy and love.

Why do we do this? Aside from our natural inclination to care deeply about little ones, it is a proven fact that children who can rely on this supportive consistency will be able to bounce back from life's inevitable bumps. A child who learns that life's hardships are not the end of the road and that there is always a tomorrow will grow up to be resilient. Developing resiliency is an important factor in how successful a person's life will be. People who learn to tackle challenges—and to bounce back from them feeling good about themselves—are more likely to be successful in their quest for a happy life.

Nutrition and Fitness

Children need not only academic and emotional support, but also attention to their physical well-being. Healthy habits and proper nutrition support the child's physical needs.

At HAFHA, exercise becomes daily fun, with activities such as jumping rope, stretching, and a wide variety of ball games.

Children also learn proper manners in order to become socially acceptable and learn why politeness is a desirable quality. Not only do they learn to get what they want by using their manners, they learn that good manners make them and others feel good.

Visone Method teachers also educate children about how to care for their bodies—washing their hands, brushing their teeth, etc. Age-appropriate discussions about their bodies follow accordingly.

Finally, a good, balanced diet and information about nutrition and health is offered to promote the child's overall well-being.

Music and Drama

When we hear the beat of our mother's pulse in the womb, we first discover music. For a young child, music is as basic as the air he breathes and is at the very foundation of how he learns. Children are natural-born music lovers; they often create their own songs as they go about their activities.

The incredible importance of music in a young child's curriculum should not be dismissed; however, it is a tragic fact that it often is. Elementary schools faced with a budget crunch often cut music programs—the very heart of their curriculum. This is most unfortunate. We now know that a lesson set to a rhythm will stick with a child more concretely than one presented by rote. It is also a fact that young children enrolled in music programs (be it learning or appreciating) score higher on reading and math tests than those who are not! (Two noted studies that back this up are the 1992 Gfeller study and the 1991 Standley and Hughes study.)

The Visone Method is an enormous supporter of music and drama every day and in every classroom. There are a number of reasons why we are so adamant about this:

1. Music draws out children who may otherwise be reticent to participate in activities.

In one incident at HAFHA, an infant in our care was being rocked to sleep as she was gently sung to. Amazingly, she sang the words back to us, even though she was less than one year old! We later discovered she was autistic, and music was the best way for her to connect and stay focused.

In another incident, a shy child would not participate in activities … until we introduced her to music, which made her smile in a big way.

Another child had disabilities, but loved singing. He would literally light up when it was music time. He eventually wrote a song that we still use. While this student has now graduated, he still comes to visit and is very proud to hear his song still being sung.

Still other children do not speak English and may be shy around those who therefore do not understand them. However, when taught some songs in English, these children blossom, coming out of their isolated shells.

2. Music and drama help children discover their special talents and allow for different ranges of participation.

There are numerous opportunities for children to excel when they participate in a classroom production: from acting, singing, and dancing to helping coordinate sets and props, to writing the script. A classroom production creates an environment where every child's special talent is showcased. Because the range of possible participation extends from simply listening and observing to full-on, active involvement, it is possible to respect each child's comfort level as he or she slowly (or quickly) moves through the spectrum of participation.

3. Children benefit enormously from role-playing.

When children role-play, they try on different personas, becoming people they may not have understood before. This increases their ability to empathize with other cultures and personalities. When a child takes on the role of a character, that child builds an imaginary picture of who that character is. As he or she tries on different moods and feelings, the door is opened to much broader understanding.

4. Language is easier to process and learn when a melody is employed to carry the words.

As infants, we prepare for the spoken word in the same way we respond to music. A child's vocabulary will quickly expand, because music and language have similar roots.

5. Being involved in a performance teaches children critical skills, increases self-esteem, and provides the opportunity to learn lifelong lessons.

Children involved in a performance practice their observation skills through concentrating on the action in the performance. Self-discipline improves, allowing the child to monitor his own behavior.

Cheering on fellow performers or helping each other learn lines and stage directions increases social skills. When children perform together, they must practice their cooperation skills so they can work together as a team. Being part of a group also increases their sense of community.

Verbal and listening skills—as well as memorization skills—are enhanced by learning lines or practicing songs. Performance also provides the opportunity to learn analytical and spatial skills. A child must analyze if a song was too fast or slow, low or loud.

Diction and projection skills are honed, giving children an edge over children who do not get the opportunity to speak or perform in public. (Public speaking skills become more critical as children reach higher grades and eventually enter the job market.)

Large motor skills are exercised as children pantomime, clap to the beat, move to the music, or sweep across the stage as they perform, which leads to better body control. Controlling hand movements or concentrating on standing straight in front of an audience increases body awareness.

Self-esteem, poise, and confidence grow along with body awareness. Shyness dissipates as children try on different guises and dance or sing their thoughts and ideas, rather than just speak them. When they hear applause from an audience and are the focus of praise from their families, their self-esteem, poise, and confidence can't help but improve!

Performing provides exposure to one of life's greatest pleasures—the beauty and passion associated with the arts. Even the lives of children who will not use dramatic skills professionally will be enriched by this early exposure to dance, opera, concerts, and plays. Through participation, children learn musical concepts and learn to identify instruments, beats, rhythms, keys, and pitch. These skills will enhance their listening pleasure and lifelong musical appreciation.

6. The rhythm produced by speech, music, and movement work together to connect sensory and motor areas in the infant's brain.

When the same songs are sung to infants over and over, the infant learns to recognize them. As the infant plays with sounds, nerve connections to the larynx are created. Brain research shows that children who have early music training have earlier cortical development. According to the 1997 Kotulak study, a child must play with sounds, even crying sounds, in order to create the motor connections that are critical to learning language.

7. Music strengthens the bond between an infant and the teacher.

Teachers can be spontaneous with infants and toddlers. Rather than rely solely on known songs, adults can make up songs about the baby's daily routine. Infant caregivers can sing about eating breakfast, having a diaper changed, transitioning to a new activity, or looking at that cute baby in the mirror. Singing to infants in this way not only develops early language, but motor skills, as they follow along with the caregiver's hand movements. Songs also strengthen the bond between baby and teacher.

8. Music has the power to heal.

Yet another reason music is so important in children's lives is its unabashed power to heal. Studies show it can lower blood pressure and reduce metabolism and respiration rates, thereby decreasing stress and increasing endorphins—which helps to quiet the nerves, as well as relieve pain, anxiety, and depression (David M. Mazie, 1996). Music therapists are often employed to help patients suffering from illnesses or malaise. Music therapists also work toward improving academic and communication skills, decreasing inappropriate behavior, increasing attention span, and strengthening leisure and social skills ... qualities a Visone Method school instills in its students.

9. Music is a natural mood enhancer.

Music calms and focuses the mind. Need to settle down? Some quiet music will help set the stage. Need to amp up? Turn up the beat. Trying to involve a shy child? Move the music activities outdoors, where she may feel less inhibited.

10. Music creates a unique bond among students.

One pilot program integrated exceptional and non-exceptional young children alike in music play, so that exceptional children can begin to be mainstreamed. Researchers found that through music play, these two diverse learning groups found common ground, which fostered healthy social interaction between them. The Greenberg and Scott studies (1989) also found that music was critical to the development of all children, exceptional as well as non-exceptional. Teachers privy to this study observed that dance movement activities provided opportunities for students with extremely different levels of ability to relate to one another and have fun together.

11. Music and drama are fun, and learning through fun makes learning easier.

Can you see now why we believe so strongly in music and drama as part of every program, every day? It's not how well children sing a song or say their lines in a play that matters—it's the tremendous benefits music and drama offer each child.

Art

Art programs are another part of many public schools' curriculum these days that are often found on the chopping block. No longer do all schools employ specially trained art instructors as a regular course of curriculum. Sadly, the young children enrolled in these schools are missing out on one of the most wonderful forms of self-expression.

A Visone Method school recognizes the importance of art in the curriculum, giving it a place of honor. At HAFHA, our students' art creations are framed and matted as "gallery" pieces. We then sponsor an art "happening" at a local gallery, where the children's work is installed and shown right alongside the work of professional artists.

Three views of early childhood art education have prevailed over the past half-century. One looks at art during these developmental stages as purely a reflection of the child's inner self. A second says early childhood art is a cognitive reflection of what children have learned about the world around them. The third perspective says young children express themselves and communicate with the larger world around them through their art. All three are probable and important, and they speak to the reasons The Visone Method values art as part of the curriculum:

1. *Not only is art pure joy to create, but a teacher doing an art project with a child can observe many things about that child that might go unnoticed otherwise.*

For example, is the child drawing dark scenarios involving family members, which could indicate emotional problems that need to be explored? Art is a form of creative expression that absorbs, stimulates, and relaxes the child. One of the most important aspects of art is that it allows the creator to express emotions. This is especially helpful for young children who may not have developed other avenues of communication yet.

2. *With art, a child's self-esteem soars.*

Like drama and music, art may become an area in which a child excels, allowing him to feel great about himself. Art is an important part of development. It helps children feel they are competent and personally powerful: "Hey, look at what I can do! I made this!"

3. *Art helps children progress through the different developmental stages.*

For example, a three-year-old begins to make the connection that the marks he makes on paper can represent objects found in the real world, while a four-year-old adds more detail to his art images as he strives to make it look "real" to his eye. A kindergartener may be able to solve the problem of how to keep drippy paint from running down her masterpiece.

When parents meet with Visone Method teachers during parent-teacher conferences, they are given a portfolio of their child's art projects, showing a progression of the child's focus and growth through attention to developmental details.

4. *Creating art provides the opportunity to use and develop a wide range of skills.*

Creating art is a cognitive process that allows the artist to solve problems (for instance, how much glue to squeeze out of a tube), predict what might happen "if," experiment with cause and effect as well as geometric design (math), and consider perspective. A young child who wants to draw a cat must remember what a cat looks like, as well as think through where to place the eyes in relationship to the nose and ears.

5. Through art, children also get to manipulate and investigate a variety of tools and materials, so science and motor skills come into play as well.

Painting on a big piece of paper placed on a standing easel, little artists develop large motor skills as they sweep back and forth with broad strokes. Trying to master holding onto a paintbrush between fingertips increases hand-eye coordination and engages the fine motor skills—arm and finger muscle coordination is needed to be able to write, whether with a mouse or pencil.

6. Art helps children develop an aesthetic sense, giving them balance.

As with drama and music, whether or not a child becomes a professional artist may be irrelevant. Experience with art expands of her world. A learned appreciation of art and beauty enrich the environment in which she grows.

7. Displaying artwork creates additional teaching opportunities.

Art in the classroom can teach children the primary colors, as well as the subtleties of hues and tones. Other themes that can be covered include shapes, shading, landscapes, portraits, sculpture, and the properties of watercolors, acrylics, oils, and pastels.

Too often, educators of young children underestimate, or aren't trained to understand, the importance of art education for young children. It is up to the teacher in the classroom to guide the child's experiences and growth in art. An appreciation of the arts (which includes music and performance, as well as the visual arts) can only benefit young minds. Children rely on the adults in their lives for access to materials, project guidance, and encouragement as their natural artistic abilities unfold in a nurturing environment.

One way Visone Method teachers stand out is in their discussion of art with their students: How did the child create the art piece? What types of materials were used? They also discuss famous artists and art history.

Children who are exposed only to "cookie cutter" art projects with rigid guidelines are missing out: these activities do not encourage experiential art skills or the appreciation of meaningful art that grows from a creative spirit.

Literacy

Is it important for young children to know how to write? Let's answer it this way: is there any function they will perform as adults where writing is *not* important? From grocery lists to love letters, from e-mails to research papers, good writing skills will give children an edge as adults who communicate with business associates, family members, and community members, whether as a car mechanic or astronaut. Even very young children spend time figuring out which words will help them achieve desired results.

Resources such as books, newspapers, and magazines and activities like writing and increasing vocabulary through discussion and listening help children discover language and its many uses. Children need to be encouraged to talk together in groups and to take turns listening, to write and tell short stories, to think of a theme and engage in literacy activities around that theme.

Writing activities in the early grades give children a head-start on making connections between letters, sounds, words, sentences, and eventually whole books. Children who are given writing and reading activities at very young ages test more successfully throughout their academic lives.

Another benefit of teaching young children early literacy skills is that they often help each other learn and take turns listening to each other, thereby creating a collaborative environment with their peers.

The brain centers for language grow rapidly as children listen, talk, and mimic more complex conversations and writing. Children should be exposed to unfamiliar, intriguing, and useful words. Teachers should become familiar with books they will read to the class, previewing stories to be read aloud and choosing new words with which to open a class discussion.

As a child's literacy develops, it becomes more obvious that writing is a visual representation of the writer's thoughts as much as painting is of the artist's. By continually refining their writing, children develop critical thinking skills and begin to define (and redefine) themselves as writers.

Journals are an excellent activity for beginning writers of all abilities, because they incorporate all aspects of literacy: reading, writing, and language development. Children can write on a variety of themes, from personal experience to creative expression. They can write about what they did over the weekend one day and create original poems the next day.

Young children have a lot to say, and expressing themselves through writing helps them focus their thoughts, increase their vocabulary, develop a lifelong love of words, and ensure a lifetime of literacy success.

Science

"Sciencing" is a new term in early childhood education. It refers to the development of a foundation of knowledge in science through discovery and experimentation. Science education is now defined as manipulating, observing, thinking, and drawing conclusions. The three goals for sciencing with young children are:

1. To develop each child's natural curiosity about the world around him

2. To broaden each child's investigative, procedural, and thinking skills

3. To increase each child's knowledge of the natural world in which she lives

Through science, young children learn the basic skills needed to explore: observation, comparison, sorting, and organizing. Understanding of these skills and basic scientific concepts expands as the child gets older. For instance, comparing living and nonliving things eventually helps young scientists learn to respect their environment.

As in music, teachers do not have to be scientists in order to perform science experiments in the classroom. Their role is often supportive, guiding the children's experience as they explore, develop patience to observe changes, and learn to ask open-ended questions.

Science instills in the young scientist a sense of wonder in the world. Learning how and why things work increases brain connections and trains the brain to solve problems. A variety of topics and themes should be incorporated into the scientific curriculum—color, acids and bases, cells, weather, bugs—there is wide array of topics to choose from.

A young child starting preschool brings curiosity into the classroom through a biological predisposition to learn. This means children are highly engaged as they explore. A little scientist increases his knowledge base through science programming. Can there be a more important reason to teach this subject to young children?

Foreign Language

Learning a second language opens doors and creates myriad opportunities for all children. Let's look at some of the benefits of learning a second language at a young age.

1. *Simply introducing a second language supercharges a child's brainpower and gives the child a measurable advantage in school.*

   Studies have shown that children who receive even a small amount of second-language instruction are more creative and better at solving complex problems (Rafferty, 1986; Garfinkel & Tabor, 1991; Armstrong & Rogers, 1997). Research also shows that elementary school children who learn second languages score higher on standardized tests (Connecticut Council of Language Teachers, 1996). When it's time for college, high school students who have studied a foreign language score higher on both the verbal and math SATs. In fact, their scores go up with each additional year of language study.

2. *It gives children a competitive edge in the real world and offers career advantages when they grow up.*

   Young people who speak a second language have an advantage in today's job market. After all, a great many Americans speak languages other than English. Knowing a second language has become a necessity in today's world. The lawyer or teacher who speaks Spanish, the doctor who speaks Italian, the marketing executive who speaks French, the plumber, hotel manager, or retailer with a second language—they're the ones who will be hired first. The world belongs to the person with the ability to communicate in more than one language. In government, business, technology, education, communications, health care, and many other areas, the opportunities are limitless for the person who grows up speaking a second language.

3. *It fosters a world of personal fulfillment and respect for other cultures.*

Comfort in another language and familiarity with other cultures, along with some knowledge of the country in which the language originated, will make your child an enthusiastic participant in the global community. It also aids in building respect for our diverse and interesting world. Travel is more meaningful and relationships more satisfying when you speak the language. This vast universe becomes smaller and within reach when you have more knowledge.

4. *Learning a second language helps boost a child's confidence and increases self-esteem.*

The Visone Method believes children at the four-year-old level, like little sponges, soak up any language they are exposed to. Such children proudly use their rapidly expanding knowledge in creative new ways as their self-esteem blooms. Vocabularies blossom as they learn to name colors, days of the week, months, the objects in their home and environment, and the calendar numbers in a new language. If asked, "Do you want to sing this song in Italian or English?" the child's answer is almost always the same: in the foreign language, because it's fun!

Like knowing a secret code, a second language is a real confidence booster for boys and girls. Parents tell us how proud their children are of their new language skills as they hold dinner conversations in their second language. Grandparents and family members across the globe enthusiastically receive phone calls and listen with a smile to greetings from their bilingual little ones, who are eager to show off their skill.

Learning a language is fun, and this attitude toward education can spill over into other areas of study.

5. *As children learn to listen and think in two languages, they develop important skills that will help them succeed in school and in life.*

Learning a second language allows young children to develop the focus and attention span that will be crucial to their academic achievements. Speaking a second language reinforces words and concepts learned in English and rewards the child with an enriched vocabulary and improved communications skills in not one, but two, languages.

Learning a second language also stretches a child's cognitive ability, leading to improved performance in many subject areas. Research shows that learning a second language improves performance in social studies, develops critical thinking skills, and enhances creativity (Landry, 1974; Hakuta, 1990).

Children who are given the chance to learn a second language become good listeners, develop excellent memory skills, and learn to see patterns in new material. These are all vital skills for learning new concepts and for overall academic success.

Children ages five to eight years old are eager to expand their knowledge of a second language because they enjoy conversing with their classmates using their newfound language. Unfortunately, most schools in America wait until middle school or high school to first introduce languages. That's too late, because it misses the "window of opportunity" (up to the age of twelve) when language acquisition is natural. Just think back to when you were first exposed to a second language in middle or high school, probably through memorization and rote learning. In contrast, young children pick up another language effortlessly by playing games and singing throughout the curriculum.

Children use their natural ear for language to absorb the accent, the rhythm, and the vocabulary of one language as easily as the next. Speaking a foreign language early, for instance in a pre-kindergarten program, makes it easier to learn another language later on as the child progresses to kindergarten and higher grades. It is all about mastering the basics of the first language, which then makes it easy to move on to the next language.

If you are questioning whether a second language might confuse your youngster, know that all children are born with a natural ability to learn languages and to keep the two (or more) distinct. Young children learn language naturally—intuitively—and with much enthusiasm and enjoyment. Notice how children who grow up in bilingual homes speak both languages automatically, without a trace of an accent.

The Visone Method confidently proposes that the earlier you introduce a second language, the more quickly and easily a child will master it, especially when the language is approached in a fun, creative, and hands-on manner. We also strongly feel that early exposure to a foreign language is one of the pivotal ways to secure a child's future.

Technology

While technology for young children is finally being recognized as a necessary part of every curriculum, The Visone Method has respected its importance for many years.

Our children are growing up in a world dominated by computers and other technological advances. Society's reliance on these advances will only increase. In order for our children to grow up to be competitive on a global platform, they will have to be accomplished in the most current technological uses.

Researchers have reported developmental gains in young children who are accustomed to computers as opposed to children who are not (Power On: commissioned by the U.S. Congress, 1997). Standardized testing scores were six points higher in some cases. Nonverbal skills, long-term memory, manual dexterity, verbal skills, problem solving, and conceptualizing skills were also higher in "tech" kids.

Improved motor skills and math concepts, as well as increased creativity, higher thinking skills, and language skills, are just some of the benefits exposure to technology offers. In addition, as one study found out (Nastasi and Clements, 1994), teaching computers and technology in the classroom leads to children believing they have the ability to affect their environment.

Also, using technology can promote some social skills. A young child who may be too shy to sit at the computer and use a program will, however, lean over the shoulder of another child "playing" on the computer and talk about the program on the screen.

A Visone Method classroom for preschool and older children has a library of programs and CDs available for children to use. These include early keyboarding, read-alongs, foreign languages, thinking games, phonics, etc. Children are taught that computers are a tool—not a toy! Rules for proper computer use (e.g., no eating or drinking near the computer) are taught right along with simple programs, definitions, and procedures. Accommodations are made to distinguish programs used for three-and-four-year-olds versus students in kindergarten or older.

In order for children to learn about technology in the classroom, teachers also need to be willing to learn and keep current with technology. They, after all, set an example for their students.

Multiple Synergies

While each program within the curriculum is important in and of itself, individual value increases as they all work together.

Considering all the educational and developmental programs a child should be exposed to, it's deeply rewarding to know these elements work together synergistically. The child who is busy building with blocks is not only learning how to stack and conceive of mathematical concepts, but is learning cause and effect—if he knocks against his building, it will fall. Can he solve the problem of how to make his architectural creation stand better? At the same time, he is also developing his motor skills.

Each area of learning overlaps with another, intertwining and crossing over. Visone Method teachers are educated in the subtleties of synergistic teaching. A walk in nature to observe firsthand how plants grow may result in picking up a seedpod and transforming it into a musical instrument or a tool to use in art projects.

Science lessons can help children with their communication skills as they share results of projects and experiments. A little scientist also increases his vocabulary, makes mental pictures of the experiment's outcome, and trains himself to increase his focus (a skill that will come in handy throughout his life).

Outdoors at playtime, children are learning about earth and physical sciences as they go up and down slides, exercising their muscles.

Collecting rocks, small toy trains, charms, and more can help a child learn about sequencing, sorting, and math. Collections can be arranged in a variety of artistic ways, furthering learning on yet another level. Add a microscope so that children can look at their collections more closely, and you've included the elements of focus and observation. Hand out cameras to the children so they can photograph their collections.

Children weave the fabric of their lives from the tools they are given by adults. A Visone Method school knows how to mix these tools for maximum benefit.

Chapter 4

The Visone Method's Classroom—How We Treat One Another

Near and dear to our hearts—and an important component of The Visone Method—is a peaceful classroom, one that builds a sheltering cocoon around the children within.

Today, perhaps more than ever before, children need to be able to come to a classroom that embraces a peaceful environment. Since 9/11, television news and other media have been filled with talk of terrorism-based violence. Children are also bombarded with violent messages from seemingly innocent cartoons, movies, and video games. Some children even witness violence right in their own neighborhoods.

For the children growing up in this new world, the reality is that violent language and behavior surrounds them. The ideal would be to change society so that our precious young children do not face the stresses of violence. However, this is not an easy task to accomplish. So where do we begin? We must let children know this is not how the world *should* be or *needs* to be. We must teach children how to resolve conflict and show them that there are alternatives to violence, fighting, and war.

The Visone Method has taken up the torch to promote Peaceful Classrooms. A Peaceful Classroom builds trust, and trust allows room for discovery, acceptance, and learning.

As people who care for and about young children, we know it is our duty to be vigilant. The societal acceptance of violence has become both very bold and very subtle. In 1984, the Federal Communications Commission deregulated children's programming. Since then, the quantity of violent content has escalated.

Some parents who say they are nonviolent buy into the concept of violence by giving their small children lunchboxes and T-shirts with crass characters and sayings. This kind of merchandise has become standard fare in stores and homes across the nation. Often, these negative messages spill over into the classrooms of our youngest children. The message is not lost on our littlest ones (remember, they *are* little sponges).

Children learn right from wrong from the adults in their lives. In the classroom, children should be able to rely on the teacher to keep them safe. Visone Method teachers and staff practice peacekeeping methods in the classroom, methods that the children can take home with them and apply to their lives outside of school.

Killing is Never a Game

Toys can be valuable tools to prepare young children for the grownup world. However, according to a *New York Times* survey (2002), the sale of toys dropped 2 percent recently because "children are getting older, younger."

Video games, the Internet, and other technological gadgets are given to children at younger and younger ages. This unto itself would not be a concern, except for what the children are being exposed to and then conclude as a result: violent messages are the accepted norm. The inappropriate content of these games overshadows any benefits, such as hand-eye coordination, a child gains from using the technology.

We can't pretend that violence doesn't exist and stick our heads in the sand, hoping we won't have to face these tough issues. Especially in the classroom, we must give children support when a family member has been victimized by violence. However, we must also put this grownup topic into perspective.

Killing is not a game. To feature it in a game treats it too casually—or, on the other hand, glorifies it. Either way, it sends the message that life has little value and desensitizes children to real-life violence. No wonder crime rates are up.

Allowing innocent babes to play games that feature violence and murder will not foster a healthy perspective. A Visone Method classroom would no more tolerate violent games than it would allow physical violence.

The Visone Method also does not condone pretend gunplay—toy guns and even "finger" guns are strictly prohibited. Guns kill. Children must learn this simple lesson early on. Children use play to try on grownup behaviors, as well as to try out new skills and role-playing. What kind of adults will children become if they think guns are toys? It is important that parents remain vigilant so that what their children learn in school is reinforced at home. Violent so-called superheroes should be banned; powerful real-life heroes should be substituted—scientists, teachers, firefighters.

Choose toys that stretch the child's imagination and creativity vs. toys that do the work for the child or expose him to video games that feature violence. The graphics associated with violent games are very vivid.

Research shows that children who play these games mimic the characters instead of using their imaginations (K. Thompson, 2001).

The violent culture our children are exposed to has an enormously negative impact on their psyches. In contrast, clay, paint, paper, costume boxes, musical instruments, construction toys, and the like complement your child's development as she wonders, "What can I do with this?"

Planet Peace

The learning environment at school *must* feel safe. The reason The Visone Method strives for a Peaceful Classroom is simple: children who are stressed by factors beyond their young control will not learn or fare well on any level. Without the aid of deeply caring teachers to help turn their feelings around and lacking the experience and vocabulary to express themselves, fearful children develop low self-worth. Therefore, it is of prime importance that the classroom be a safe, nurturing environment where children are happy to be and happy to learn.

Children learn best in an environment that offers support and predictability. Happy, safely nested children are easier to teach. A Peaceful Classroom allows them to interact comfortably with others and builds upon positive, empowering interactions.

The Visone Method guides children toward getting along with the community of other children in their classroom. The children in the classroom live and work together each day. We like to think of the classroom as the children's own "planet," where everyone gets along and is respectful of each other.

Of course, as in the real world, not everyone will get along every day. This is where a teacher can truly effect change, role-modeling behavior that creates a peaceful, positive atmosphere in the room. We may not always agree with each other—this is normal. *How* we work out our disagreements is the key; they should be resolved with respect, kindness, and manners. These behaviors are not always easy to put into practice, and this is where seasoned Visone Method teachers shine—by demonstrating, through actions and words, how to resolve conflict and keep peace appropriately.

Resolving Conflict

Showing young children better ways to manage or sidestep conflicts—in the classroom, in the neighborhood, or at home—is essential. A Visone Method teacher will model ways to state feelings without becoming violent or using harmful language. Children learn through these behaviors that the outcome of resolving conflict peacefully is positive: all parties win.

Before children can put conflict resolution techniques into practice, they need to be taught some rules about safety and classroom procedures—and the reasons for these rules. They should also be exposed to the cultures of others. In addition, they should be allowed a place to discuss their own fears and what they need to feel safe in the classroom.

Children look to the adults in their lives to keep them safe and to be respectful of their feelings. Children who feel safe to talk about their fears with the adults in their lives can feel comfortable in their Peaceful Classroom.

A Visone Method teacher speaks to their students respectfully, including them in decision-making at age-appropriate levels and helping them to use good judgment. Teaching these important lessons benefits the teacher as well as the child: a classroom filled with respectful children is focused. A teacher can teach more effectively when children behave respectfully.

Visone Method teachers initiate lessons about conflict resolution by using developmentally appropriate language and concepts every child can grasp. When there is a conflict, teachers try to understand each child's perspective. In the case of conflict with another child, both children are given time to tell their story without being interrupted.

Another way to teach children to be peacemakers is to help them develop compassion and responsibility. Allowing them the opportunity to say "I'm sorry" when they have misbehaved accomplishes this.

When children are taught why they should be sorry for hitting, yelling, being rude, or being defiant, they develop compassion and the ability to see things from others' perspectives, culturally, religiously, and politically. Voicing their newfound compassion means they take responsibility for their actions. Children can then understand why shoving someone in the playground, bossing a sibling around, or hitting a classmate is unacceptable.

Young ones in a Peaceful Classroom learn how to be peacemakers on Planet Peace, and the problem-solving skills these children learn at a young age will remain with them as they grow into adults.

We cannot entirely shelter children from violence, but we must do everything we can to teach them that there are alternatives. The Visone Method firmly believes that the world can change one community at a time, one family at a time—one child at a time. While we pray that the world will enjoy global peace, we try to care for our little corner of the world, which means caring for our children in a Peaceful Classroom environment.

PART II
EVIDENCE SUPPORTING THE VISONE METHOD

Chapter 5

Scientific Support for The Visone Method: The Carnegie Study on Early Childhood Education

The Visone Method of excellence in early childhood education started out as a philosophy. As with all good philosophies, it is essential to have hard research to back it up, give it credence, and underscore its value.

In 1996, as The Visone Method was being quietly and successfully put to the test in New Jersey at HAFHA, the internationally respected Carnegie Corporation's Task Force on Learning in the Primary Grades released their findings in a study entitled, "Years of Promise."

This eye-opening report, published by such a highly prestigious independent organization, revealed to the world the undeniable importance of *quality* early childhood education. The report's findings were striking in their similarity to what was already being practiced at HAFHA. Most importantly, it revealed the enormous impact a superior early education has on future academic successes and quality of life.

The Carnegie Corporation

Many Americans are familiar with Andrew Carnegie, a celebrated philanthropist who was the first to state publicly that "all personal wealth beyond that required for the needs of one's family" should be in trust for the benefit of the community.

Carnegie was a man who literally put his money where his mouth was. At age sixty-five, he sold his steel company for $480 million and devoted the rest of his life to philanthropic activities and writing. Carnegie's lifelong passion was to help ensure a quality education for all. He worked tirelessly to establish free public libraries.

For over 100 years, the Carnegie Corporation has supported education that makes long-term contributions. Its stated goal is to increase access to a rich, quality education that will "prepare students for success in today's knowledge-based economy."

The Carnegie Corporation's concerns include building a deep capacity for literacy and analytic and interpretive skills, the "essential importance" of quality teaching, and a commitment to "high standards that serve students."

For their studies, the Carnegie Corporation consulted the nation's leading practitioners and researchers. Of major interest to the Carnegie Corporation is increasing adolescent academic skills, including reading, which are still shown to be very poor in the middle school and beyond. Findings stress the extreme, immediate importance of *quality early education*, such as outlined in this book.

The "Years of Promise" Study

The Carnegie Corporation's "Years of Promise" study on early childhood education supports and mirrors The Visone Method. In a nutshell, it found that when children are presented with challenging learning opportunities in an environment of loving acceptance, they will excel.

When the report was first published, we at HAFHA realized that our "philosophy" was indeed respected and credibly researched. We now had concrete proof that our efforts to ensure the best possible education for each young student pay off. Placing early childhood students in challenging situations means they will excel academically and socially as they make their transition to higher grades—and beyond into adult life.

As practiced at HAFHA and supported by the "Years of Promise" study, hands-on opportunities in language, math, science, creative movement, music, drama, and computer education invite children to reach their highest potential. This should become the blueprint for all early childhood education.

The "Quiet Crisis"

The first component of the Carnegie Corporation's "Years of Promise" study we'll look at is entitled "The Quiet Crisis." It reports that children under the age of three and their families are in trouble, due in large part to anxiety about inadequate child care and early education opportunities.

Three years before the report was published, the National Educational Goals Panel issued the startling statistic that almost half the infants and toddlers in the United States start life at a "disadvantage and do not have the supports necessary to grow and thrive."

The Goals Panel further stated that children three and under typically confront one or more major risk factors, including those identified here:

- **Inadequate prenatal care.** Nearly one quarter of pregnant women do not receive prenatal care. "The risk of delivering a ... baby with ... intellectual difficulties is greater when ... a woman does not receive adequate prenatal care."

- **Isolated parents and community violence.** More divorced and single parents combined with less family and community support have isolated parents raising young children. In addition, most children are victims of some form of exposure to violence. No longer is any community immune.

- **Substandard child care.** "With over half of new mothers returning to jobs within a year of their child's arrival, many infants and toddlers are in substandard child care [our definition would also include inadequacies in physical stimulation, academics, socialization, and nurturing] 35-plus hours per week."

- **Insufficient attention.** Many parents do not give their young children's intellectual needs their due: only half of infants and toddlers are read to with any regularity by their parents. As a result, teachers reported that only one in three kindergarteners arrive in school ready to learn.

The National Educational Goals Panel went on to identify four key "dimensions of school readiness:"

1. Physical well-being and motor development

2. Social and emotional development

3. Language usage

4. The mastering of "learning styles that allow children to approach new tasks and challenges effectively"

The Carnegie Task Force on Meeting the Needs of Young Children, in response to the Goals Panel research, summed these facts up as a "quiet crisis" and urged a national response.

The Critical Importance of the First Three Years

Calling particular attention to the "critical importance" of the first three years of life, the Carnegie Task Force defines these years as the crucial "starting point." It reminds readers that how "individuals function from the preschool years, even through adulthood, hinges to a significant extent" on the experiences children have in their first three years.

New, sophisticated technology, including brain scans, allowed researchers to identify how a baby's brain develops. Their five key findings are powerful:

1. The brain development realized during the prenatal period and first year of life is more rapid and extensive than had been previously thought.

2. Brain development is much more vulnerable to environmental influence than was previously believed.

3. The influence of the early environment on development is *long lasting*.

4. Environment affects the number of brain cells and connections, as well as how these connections are "wired."

5. Early stress impacts brain function in a negative way.

The good news? While an adverse environment can compromise a young child's brain function and development, putting the child at greater risk of developing cognitive, behavioral, and physical problems, a "good start in life can do more to promote learning," as well as prevent damage, than had ever been imagined. Other positive contributing factors to a good start in life include dependable caregivers utilizing appropriately positive practices and a safe, supportive community.

The study also concluded, as The Visone Method stresses, that parents are the child's first teacher. "Sensitive, nurturing parenting provides children with a sense of trust that allows them to feel confident in exploring the world." Touching, holding, talking, and reading to infants and toddlers are most effective for later development.

Unfortunately, the study also showed that economic pressures on families to bring in double incomes translates to less time with children than parents of only one generation earlier. Parents resent the loss of family time and are also exhausted and overloaded. Complicating this issue is the rarely family-friendly workplace. The study also found that "too often, substandard child care and preschools *actually undermine* a child's healthy development."

However, a *quality* early childhood educational facility can fill in the gaps a parent is unable to fill, compensating in large part for parental absence and lack of parenting time. A quality early childhood educational facility will actually help parents strengthen the bond with their children by creating opportunities, as HAFHA does, for parent and child to share time. They will also keep parents informed about their child's day and developmental progress.

Promote Responsible Parenthood

The Carnegie Corporation's "Years of Promise" study on early childhood education also called for promoting responsible parenthood: as the report refers to it, "the most critical starting point."

A long-time advocate of parents as a child's first, best teacher, The Visone Method agrees wholeheartedly with this finding: "childrearing is inseparable from daily domesticity." In other words, it is impossible to take parents out of the picture when it comes to child development. The kind of care parents give children and the framework they create for later learning "spring from the rhythms" of the child's home life.

The study acknowledges that parenting is a lifetime commitment, entailing at least two decades of "sustained attention." The study also concludes that it is "difficult to imagine an enterprise that has a greater impact on public life" than parenting—meaning the productivity of our citizenry, vitality of our culture, and strength of our public institutions.

The study also reiterates its findings that the time, energy, and resources parents give to their children will influence the children's success.

The stated goal of the Task Force study was not to tell parents how to parent, but rather to identify what support and information parents need to parent well, leading them to "sound choices."

When parents parent well, their children are more likely to "meet life with optimism, competence, and compassion." Sadly, the study again found that the opposite is true: unprepared parents open their children to "many and serious" risks.

Drawing on this, the study determined that parents could benefit from three key areas in education, services, and support:

1. **Planned childbearing**. Encourage pregnancy under circumstances that minimize risks for children.

2. **Prenatal care and support**. With an infant's capacity for learning during early years at stake *in utero,* health education and early and ongoing risk assessment for pregnant couples is vital.

3. **Parent education and support**. While society readily acknowledges the need for job training in many areas, it "tends to act as if parenting skills should come naturally." Yet no job is more challenging.

The report urges readers to consider the circumstances new parents of infants and toddlers face. The "newness of the parental role, the child's rapid physical, intellectual, and emotional development, can make the job even more demanding and overwhelming." Any parent of an infant or toddler would likely agree.

Added to these points should be the variation in structure, values, need, and resources found in families, as well as the family's ability to seek out the support and education they need. While parenting needs exist on many levels, good parenting programs will encompass certain common elements:

- They will increase the parent's understanding of child development and parent-child relationships.

  o A quality early childhood education facility will accomplish this through their curriculum, demonstrating the type of skills children should be developing, as HAFHA does.

  o The Visone Method shows that a quality early childhood education facility can help parents develop strong bonds with their children in several ways, including parent-child events and keeping parents informed about what their child is doing in the classroom so that parent and child have a starting point for discussing the child's day at school. HAFHA's monthly newsletter to parents is chock-full of details about school events and programs.

- They will provide models of positive parenting.

  o A quality early childhood education facility achieves this by teaching in a loving, nurturing environment, one of the core components of The Visone Method.

- They will establish a network of social support with other parents.

  o A quality early childhood education facility invites parents to connect with one another through a variety of events and activities, including community charity fundraising events presented at, or by, the school, as at HAFHA.

- They will establish an ongoing relationship with parents.

  o A parent-teacher conference can be invaluable to both parent and teacher as they learn more about and deepen their understanding of each other. Strengthening this key relationship means everyone is working toward the same goal to benefit the young child.

The Carnegie study also points out that appropriate staffing and training are key to successful parent education and support programs. They view this as a "preventative action."

Ensure Good Health and Protection

Your child is enrolled in a quality early childhood education program staffed by trained, intelligent, caring teachers. What else should you be concerned about?

Again, The Visone Method and the Carnegie Study on Early Childhood Education agree about the importance of the health and protection of our young children.

The study reported that few social programs guarantee longer-term benefits than those that ensure good health care for infants and toddlers. Healthy children have a greater chance of succeeding in school, becoming more productive members of the workforce, and, eventually, better parents themselves.

"We don't have to guess at the benefits of early health care," the study says. "Indeed, in no other area of social policy can costs and benefits be calculated so precisely."

Being healthy encompasses remaining safe. The study found that many young children do not grow up safely. "Some spend long stretches in substandard child care while their parents work, under the supervision of underpaid, distracted babysitters or in the care of brothers and sisters who themselves need adult attention." Some parents do not realize that the setting they provide is unsafe.

Of these recommendations, *all* are part of The Visone Method:

- Provide needed health care services for all infants and toddlers.

  o The study reports the quality of health care for children varies significantly: "Many health concerns of young children are preventable with proper care."

  o The Visone Method calls for regular nurse visits and screenings (hearing, eyesight, etc.) for young children. This becomes even more urgent as we discover, through the Carnegie study, that less than half of two-year-olds have seen a pediatrician the recommended nine times since their birth.

o   The study also reminds the reader that children with chronic or disabling conditions need "specially designed services and support."

• Protect young children from injury.

o   The study concluded that unintentional injuries remain the leading cause of death among children aged one to four. Many nonfatal injuries result in disabling conditions. Again, the study found that most of these injuries are preventable: "Promoting young children's health is a responsibility shared by parents, other caregivers and educators ..."

o   A quality school will have, in writing, specific procedures in place to protect children from injury (such as a requirement that staff be trained in CPR and first aid).

• Create safe environments.

o   The Task Force declared that it is the right of all children to grow up safely. "Energy and resources must be directed toward preventing violence in children's lives." One way this is accomplished is by appropriate positive, nurturing discipline that guides the child, as practiced by The Visone Method.

Guarantee Quality Child Care Choices

One of the important findings that came out of this study is this: "In a very real sense, parents and child care providers are jointly raising many of this nation's youngest children." As the report was being written, over five million children, three and younger, were spending the better part of their day being cared for by adults other than their own parents, while their parents worked outside of the home. Over half of these children were not in family-related child care.

The study goes on to ask, "How well is the system of child care meeting the needs of our youngest children and their families?" As had already been established, the majority of these children were in substandard child care with underpaid workers, and the children were "overstressed and unhappy," due in large part to the ratios between adult and children.

Shockingly, the study found that in many cases one adult cared for upwards of six or seven infants. On the upside, the report also noted that, "In some well-run settings, competent child care providers attend to small numbers of children." Young children in these settings experience a "happy and stimulating day."

As recommended by The Visone Method, there are never more than four infants per adult. This low ratio ensures that infants get the hands-on nurturing necessary to foster their development.

Continuing, the report further found that too many parents are forced to "make do" and accept child care that is "unreliable and unsatisfactory."

When both parents work outside of the home, they need child care in order to stay focused at work. The disruption that poor quality child care brings to these families affects everyone. It causes undue stress for parents who must provide income, and the stress eventually winds its way down to the family's young children.

Many parents "make do" because they don't know what criteria to look for when selecting a child care setting for their child.

As the study concludes, the child care crisis means that many of our youngest children miss early experiences that are necessary for the development of healthy intellectual and social capacities. "Their well-being is jeopardized by poor quality care and … a high turnover among providers." The Visone Method recognizes this important factor. Many staff members have been at HAFHA since its beginning.

The Task Force "strongly" recommends that child care choices be made a high priority. "Parents need child care arrangements that are high-quality, accessible, and affordable." The report bluntly states: "For healthy development, infants and toddlers need close relationships with a small number of caring people," including adults in child care settings.

The study defined quality child care to include young children in "small groups in environments that are safe and comfortable … each adult worker is responsible for only a few children and personnel are well prepared. The program encourages parental involvement … (and) assigns a small number of children to a sensitive, trained staff member. This goes far toward achieving individualized attention for every child ..." These words are nearly identical to those in the HAFHA manual.

The report goes on to say: "Unfortunately, these programs are the exception rather than the rule. The standards are varied, weak, or even non-existent and many states allow infants and toddlers to be cared for by providers with no specialized training and who have not even completed high school ... Even providers with some college are woefully underpaid ... Turnover for child care providers is nearly three times the rate reported by U.S. companies ... While many providers lack specific preparation, few incentives exist to encourage training; to ensure that children are nurtured, better qualified staff are essential ... This would go a long way toward improving child care services."

The report continued to echo the Visone belief that parents are the child's first best teacher by addressing the need for paid maternity/adoption leave for new parents. (At the time of the report, the United States was *not* one of 127 other nations that offered paid parental leave. Today, the Family and Medical Leave Act allows for up to twelve weeks of unpaid leave with continuing paid health insurance—if the employee had paid health insurance prior to the leave. This legislation was written for companies with fifty or more employees, thereby affecting only 60 percent of businesses in this country.)

Estimates of the value of goods and services devoted to the care and education of young children range from $120 billion to $240 billion annually, much of which is picked up by overworked parents. The report was hopeful that employers are "increasingly finding it good business" to respond to parents' needs.

Mobilize Communities to Support Young Children and Their Families

This section of "Years of Promise," the Carnegie Corporation's Study on Early Childhood Education, reviewed community services for young children and their families.

The researchers found that while some communities respond to the needs of its children, most do not: many communities are far more "responsive to the needs of their working residents than to the needs of adults caring for young children … A growing body of research supports the premise that community characteristics do indeed affect individual outcomes for children."

Following the premise that "It takes a village," the report found that a supportive social network means people in communities care about the children in their neighborhoods. Therefore, "children benefit."

By promoting a "community culture of responsibility" that includes the types and quantities of quality child care facilities in the community, "resources will be marshaled to define the needed interventions to meet specific goals." In other words, communities are encouraged to step up to the plate and shoulder a portion of the responsibility to ensure the ultimate well-being of their youngest residents.

A "Call to Action"

In its final recommendations, the "Years of Promise" study proposed a "Call to Action."

Reiterating the points made earlier, the report called upon various sectors of society to join forces to offer a "decent start in life" to young children, including the president, Congress, federal agencies, states, community leaders, philanthropic sectors, health care decision makers, service providers, business leaders, and media, offering specific recommendations to each.

In addition, educators were encouraged to work together with other community agencies to incorporate services to children under three when planning schools, as well as to educate young people about parenthood and provide more training for child care providers.

Finally, mothers and fathers were urged to do "everything in their power to secure the knowledge and resources to plan and raise children responsibly."

We assume that, as a parent, educator, child care provider, or person who cares about young children, you agree with this last statement—that's why you are reading this book.

Chapter 6
The Visone Method's TerraNova Test Results

In order to be successful, an education must provide relevant, measurable results. This was the thinking behind putting The Visone Method to the test.

In the more than ten years The Visone Method has been put into practice at our own Home Away From Home Academy, we've been able to observe and research through personal, hands-on experience just how young children learn and develop. For example, we have learned that infants need appropriate stimulation to jump-start their brainpower, that toddlers' emerging independence and mobility translate into increased skills, that preschoolers and pre-kindergarteners absorb learning like thirsty sponges, and that first-and second-graders can barely contain their excitement when they are being taught a new concept.

In order to prove that The Visone Method is both valid and effective, we wanted to put it to the test. Our research into testing alternatives led us to the recognized independent testing firm CTB/McGraw-Hill and their TerraNova Performance Assessments.

Teaching materials should reflect research-based understanding of children's learning. By evaluating test results, assessments help teachers build new curriculum and select materials based on what the student has already learned. Assessment results must also be verifiable and credible when contrasted with results from other schools across the country.

About CTB/McGraw-Hill TerraNova Standardized Tests

The seventy-year-old CTB Company processes more than twenty million test documents each year. They serve thousands of school districts annually with objective reports of individual student and school strengths. CTB/McGraw-Hill is the test publisher of choice for twenty-three state departments of education.

CTB is a pioneer in the use of statistical methods. The company adheres to the Standards for Educational and Psychological Testing, the American Educational Research Association, and the National Council on Measurement in Education, among other equally reputable organizations. In addition, CTB uses an Objectives Performance Index, which provides precise measurement.

Results spell out what students have learned and retained as compared with other students in the same grade level from every imaginable corner of the country. The results can also be used to update and course-correct curriculum if needed. In the case of The Visone Method, the results underscored and verified what we had learned on our own: that our method of teaching produced bright, eager students who reach higher levels of learning than a majority of their peers.

Another reason we chose the TerraNova test is that the test itself is engaging for the test-takers. Test developers work closely with teachers, administrators, students, and parents to produce the finest skills-based examinations available.

Results are the most important element of an assessment system and should mean more than numbers. In addition to *what* children learn, test results must also express a varied and complex content that aids the school in understanding *how* the children learn, helping teachers draw reliable conclusions. A useful assessment and reporting system needs to look beyond just scores. The TerraNova's test results do just that.

Our Test Results: Just What We Thought They'd Be—Only Better

The May 2005 national achievement test scores for Home Away From Home Academy produced by TerraNova, reproduced in chart form below, very clearly spell out the effectiveness of our teaching methods on young minds.

When compared to students nationally, Visone Method students were advanced across the board:

- Kindergarteners tested at a reading level comparable to eight months into first grade (1.8) and performed math at a level equivalent to four months into second grade (2.4).

- First-graders read at a level comparable to four months into third grade (3.4) and tested at a level equivalent to nine months into fourth grade (4.9) in language arts.

- Second-graders tested at a fifth-grade level (5.5) in math and science, with stunning results in language arts, comparable to nine months into sixth grade (6.9).

Home Away From Home Academy—National Achievement Test Scores (Reflecting June 2005 School Year)

HAFHA National Grade Level Equivalents						
GRADE LEVEL	Reading	Language	Vocabulary	Math	Science	Social Studies
Kindergarten	1.8	2.5	N/A	2.4	N/A	N/A
1st Grade	3.4	4.9	3.1	3.4	2.6	2.2
2nd Grade	4.3	6.9	5.5	5.3	5.3	6.4

We are proud of our achievements. The advanced educational programs we continue to provide through The Visone Method exceed the national norms at every grade level.

The results of the Carnegie study reviewed in Chapter 5 sum it up: "The effects of a high-quality early childhood education are long-term and continue to positively predict children's school performance well into their school careers."

In the next chapter, we will see how these outstanding TerraNova test results translate when a Visone Method-taught child reaches the upper grades.

Chapter 7
What Parents Say About The Visone Method

The TerraNova assessments give credence to how much The Visone Method students excel when compared to other students in the same grade levels. The survey of former HAFHA parents expands upon that picture, demonstrating the longevity of the Method.

Over 1,000 students have experienced The Visone Method as practiced at HAFHA. How do these students do academically five or even ten years after they leave HAFHA?

In a nutshell, what students learn at HAFHA sticks with them. This is true not only because are children taught high-level academics under The Visone Method, but they also acquire the tools necessary to maintain their achievements: superb study habits, appropriate behavior techniques, commitment to learning, and a serious approach to homework.

The parents' surveys are persuasive. For example, 75 percent of former students at HAFHA continue to rank in the top 10 percentile of their class in academic performance. One quarter of former students have been placed in GATE (Gifted and Talented Education) programs. The overwhelming majority of parents attributed their children's continuing success to their early learning under The Visone Method.

The following results are based on the responses of parents of all children who attended HAFHA since 1993.

Summary of HAFHA Parent Survey

- 75 percent of former HAFHA students remain in the top 10 percent of their classes
- 25 percent are in GATE (Gifted and Talented Education) programs
- 63 percent of students continue to maintain advanced reading levels
- 60 percent continue their involvement with foreign language

- 88 percent of students report a good technological foundation at HAFHA
- 81 percent continue with music programs
- 70 percent continue with theatrical aspirations
- 89 percent maintain interest in science
- 97 percent of parents report that their children feel at ease with public speaking
- 99 percent of parents report that their children have confidence in their academic and social performance
- 98 percent say they recommend The Visone Method's strong early childhood academic foundation

Out of the Mouths of Moms and Dads

Parents also included unsolicited comments on their surveys:

- "HAFHA was the best jump start (my daughter) could have gotten."
- "Your program surpasses whatever is offered in the public schools."
- "My child excels in oral presentation thanks to HAFHA."
- "While my child should be going into fourth grade, he was advanced to fifth grade because he was given the opportunity to excel at HAFHA. He is the youngest in his class, amazing many in how he is succeeding academically and socially!"
- "My child's academic success (in public school) is attributed to being part of an environment that provided advanced academic learning opportunities and a challenging curriculum at a young age. There were many opportunities for socialization and confidence building at HAFHA."
- "She absolutely loves science and it's because of HAFHA's fun approach."
- "He loves to act on stage and is not shy (thanks to his introduction to theater at HAFHA)."

- "He is without doubt a leader in his classroom due to the confidence gained at HAFHA."

- "My child is clearly a 'big' step ahead of all the children in his grade."

- "Learning hands-on science at HAFHA was so much more beneficial than simple textbook instruction."

- "There is not one shy bone in her body. She always refers back to the plays she was in at HAFHA."

- "Both boys have great social skills and confidence in academic situations. They are both now in gifted programs."

- "My daughter had an excellent start at HAFHA, which will make her successful in her future academics."

- "She is an excellent student and might have done well anywhere, but she was able to learn much more at HAFHA in addition to the music and theater program (she wouldn't have gotten elsewhere)."

- "On the third day of public school, her teacher wanted to know where she went to preschool because she was so well prepared."

- "He is top in his class in reading and vocabulary and loves to be on stage."

Our methods have been tested, and the results are clear: The Visone Method *really* works.

PART III

THE VISONE METHOD IN ACTION: AGES 3 MONTHS THROUGH 2 YEARS

Chapter 8
The "Early Years:" An Overview

Our Youngest Charges Deserve the Best Start

What children experience in their earliest months and years profoundly impacts their entire lives. The core of a lifetime of emotional, intellectual, and physical development sets its roots during infancy and toddlerhood.

An infant is born with about 100 billion nerve cells. By the time the infant has gone through the toddler stage, almost all the nerve cells have made their connections, mapping the child's development for a lifetime.

When children are deprived of opportunities for the best emotional, intellectual, and physical start in life, they may never make it up later on. A poor environment, lack of stimulation, and a day devoid of loving attention can result in a life deprived of optimal development.

On the other hand, infants and toddlers thrive when their needs are met.

The Earliest Months and Years Really Count

Many scientific studies—including the previously discussed Carnegie study and the National Institute of Child Health and Human Development Study of Early Child Care—have shown that a child's brain develops in direct correlation to the experiences to which the child is exposed. Our own daily observations at HAFHA, backed by independent testing, underscore these results.

Studies consistently show that the earliest months and years establish the groundwork for life. As the Carnegie study found, brain development in newborns and young children is much more rapid and extensive than had been previously believed. Young children are extremely vulnerable to their environments and what they are exposed to through their surroundings. How much and how often they are stimulated and nurtured corresponds directly to how rapidly connections in the brain are made.

As the Carnegie study reports, "the quality of care received by children ... a good start in life ... can do much to promote learning and prevent damage." The Cost, Quality, and Child Outcomes Study distinguished between high-quality and low-quality child care. The children in the higher quality facilities showed more advances in language and math, were better socialized, had warm relationships with their teachers, and developed positive attitudes. (A positive attitude is one of the basic components of resiliency, the ability to bounce back from the hardships in every life). The findings repeatedly emphasize that children who experienced high-quality child care entered their school years "ready to succeed."

This is where The Visone Method excels, with professionally honed details that create the difference between high and low quality child care and early education.

Chapter 9

The Infant Program (Ages 3 Months to 14 Months)

Curriculum for Infants

The curriculum for infants has been carefully designed to fulfill the needs of the infant who is learning, as well as the caregiver who is teaching. The Visone Method stresses the five vital areas of infant learning:

1. **Social and Emotional Development:** It is amazing to see how quickly a baby will learn to smile in recognition of a familiar face or in response to a teacher's voice. Even more amazing is to watch how quickly babies learn to hand an object to a teacher and to point at or reach for an object they want. Infants also learn the very valuable socialization skills of:

    o   Responding to their own name

    o   Recognizing new faces and other babies

    o   Waving "bye-bye"

2. **Language Development:** Visone Method teachers talk to the babies in their care all day, encouraging the babies to talk back, laugh, or mimic the sound the teacher is making. Songs are sung, music is played, and books are on hand for touching and observing, as well as for reading to the children. Connections grow in the baby's brain as she is stimulated in the most optimal ways. Teachers further the baby's language development by:

    o   Encouraging the baby to listen and look at caregivers as they talk

    o   Making sounds

    o   Talking to the baby during changing time

3. **Cognitive Development:** Babies start to perceive, remember, and judge at this early age. If a teacher purposely hides an object from the baby behind her, the baby will use his skills of reason to figure out where it

is. Eye-hand coordination is developed, as are the important skills of sorting and matching, all accomplished through stimulating play that includes:

o Working on visual skills

o Watching objects in motion

o Observing and playing in front of the mirror

4. **Motor Skill Development:** Learning to hold up his chest and head while lying on his stomach gives the baby the opportunity to develop large muscles. Teachers also encourage infants to roll from a lying down position to a side position, to crawl, pull up, and sit up. Smaller muscles are likewise exercised as infants learn to grasp toys, follow moving objects, and move objects from one hand to the other. It is always exciting to see babies learn to use their index finger and thumb to pick up objects, because developing this skill is critically important to a child's writing abilities. Other ways motor skills develop large and small muscles include:

o Holding objects in each hand

o Shaking rattles and other toys

o Learning to grip

o Stopping a rolling ball with two hands

o Picking up a ball

o Stacking a two-piece toy, such as blocks

o Removing blocks from a container and putting them back

5. **Listening Skills:** Keeping the baby's listening skills alert encourages the child's later ability to learn in a classroom setting. Listening skills must be properly developed before a child can read. The Visone Method calls for teachers to expose infants to a variety of music and soothing, playful talk. All these elements add to the important work of stimulating a baby's ability to tune into and distinguish sounds. For instance:

o Listening to sounds and turning toward the source of the sound heard, such as hand clapping o   Tapping on a drum or rhythmically shaking a rattle

o   Exposure to a variety of sounds (musical instruments, toys, whistling, etc.)

In addition to a focus on the five vital areas of learning, infants at HAFHA learn to become aware of their own bodies by being encouraged to:

1. Discover their own hands, fingers, feet, and toes

2. Play games such as Pat-A-Cake and Peek-A-Boo

3. Smile

Finally, as they transition to more solid foods, infants are taught to eat finger foods, hold a cup, and use a spoon.

What the Baby's Day Looks Like Using The Visone Method

As we've already seen, an infant enters the world ready to learn, so The Visone Method requires teachers to teach. It is a known fact that children develop more rapidly during the first year of life than during any other time. In our infant program at HAFHA, our teachers hug, hold, feed, change diapers, rock, sing, read, talk, snuggle, play music, and teach simple skills to the infants in their care *every day*.

Upon arrival for the day, parents and infants are greeted with warm smiles by teachers and are given the time to say good-bye. Then, the child is guided to play, explore, and learn. Infants have time for self-directed play, such as stacking toys and blocks. As they play, caregivers verbally offer friendly encouragement.

Play is how infants learn; it is a fully absorbing experience for the child. While engaged, the babies are thinking, observing, solving problems, and familiarizing themselves with their emotions. All the while, the benefits of nurtured play with a wholly interested adult work their magic. Rolling a ball back and forth between baby and teacher helps an infant coordinate muscles and demonstrates how to play cooperatively. Introducing new toys with different textures develops the baby's tactile senses and provides the opportunity for children who learn best by touching to try things out for themselves. In addition to repetitive play, new activities are introduced on a regular basis.

At HAFHA, happy babies play and begin to vocalize. They explore and observe while crawling, sitting, listening, and responding in a stimulating environment created specifically for them. Activities for infants are designed to complement each vital development stage. For example, specific activities allow for sensory integration, such as finding the source of touch or discovering a child's own hands, feet, fingers, and toes.

Children are never too young to start being exposed to music and movement, such critically important components of each child's development. Songs and music accompany physical play as frequently as possible, since infants learn so well through rhyme and rhythm.

All daily schedules are interwoven with routine care. In the infant program, that includes diaper changing, naptime, hand washing, and fortifying, healthful snacks.

Chapter 10

The Waddler Program (Ages 15 Months to 24 Months)

By the time an infant takes his first tentative steps (what we refer to as "waddling"), he might be ready for the next developmentally appropriate program.

Having developed so quickly in so many areas under The Visone Method, an eighteen-month-old child is mastering everyday activities, including eating, turning pages in books, sipping from a cup, following simple directions, and feeding himself. These eager learners are ready for what's next.

With new stages come new responsibilities. Therefore, some waddler play enlists rules, especially when it comes to learning a new skill. The Visone Method refers to this structured type of activity as "guided play."

In the waddler program, The Visone Method sets goals for children that parallel their developmental stages. The curriculum incorporates play that is designed to meet—and exceed—these goals. (Please note: As in all developmental guidelines, the age ranges for these goals are approximate. Some children will develop more quickly than others. Check with your pediatrician if you have concerns about your own child's rate of development.)

Curriculum for Waddlers

Vital areas of development have been carefully built into the waddler program:

1. **Social and Emotional Development**
   o   Children at this age show pride in their ability to care for themselves. Therefore, they are given opportunities to choose foods they like, demonstrate possible interest in using the potty and wash hands and faces on their own.

o The Visone Method offers spontaneous opportunities for children to explore socially and emotionally. For instance, puppet play helps children express feelings they may not share otherwise.

o At this stage, children are encouraged to share play objects with each other.

o Waddlers will "check-in" with caregivers and teachers as they explore around the room, enjoying a new independence, yet not wanting to travel too far from their security base.

2. **Language Development**

o The waddler program provides numerous opportunities to further language skills. Children are asked to point to and name body parts, retrieve a specific toy or book when asked to, and communicate needs using one word.

o "Fun centers" around the waddler room aid children in communication with one another as well as with the teacher.

o Children are encouraged to talk about what they are doing, from dressing a doll to telling a felt board story.

3. **Cognitive Development**

o Cognitive skills take a big leap in the waddler program. Children are taught to reach for something beyond their grasp and learn to reason through how to go about getting it. By the time a child is between twenty months and two years old, he should be able to use his hands independently of each other.

o Drawing circles and vertical lines is a perfect activity to increase hand-eye coordination at this age.

o Simple puzzles representing body parts or shapes are now introduced.

o Children learn to stack blocks and match pairs from groups of different objects.

o They learn to put objects in their appropriate place and to pick out a circle from other shapes.

4. **Motor Skills Development**

   o   As anyone who has been around a child of waddler age knows, it is an active age! Children are given the opportunity to explore by running, walking (including sideways), sitting in a chair, and balancing on one foot. In other words, waddlers' gross motor skills are given a healthy workout.

   o   Push-and-pull toys are provided to help waddlers develop both fine and gross motor skills.

   o   Waddlers increase their fine motor skills through simple art projects. For example, waddlers are shown a stroke with a crayon and learn to imitate it.

What the Waddler's Day Looks Like Using The Visone Method

After gentle good-byes from their parents and warm welcomes from their teachers and caregivers, a waddler's day gets going with guided play. At the waddler stage of development, children love to explore via movement, crawling through safe fabric tunnels and mazes as well as climbing over and under safe toys. Weather permitting, children can play outside for development of their large muscles.

At circle time, waddlers are ready to dive into a slightly more challenging program than when they were infants. They discover the calendar, become aware of outside events, count numbers, and explore various weather conditions.

Waddlers are surrounded by lots of music and movement, including a cheerful good-morning song. One excellent way to incorporate movement into a waddler program is through a movement story, which waddlers can act out with puppets. Another excellent focus is on gross motor skills that incorporate music themes through dance, such as the waddler's popular favorite, the "Hokey Pokey." Warmup stretches help develop large muscles. The more these muscles are worked, the more large motor skills develop.

Each week and each month, themes are presented and explored that incorporate hands-on projects. Art, puzzles, and building toys pepper a waddler's schedule, updated to relate to specific weekly or monthly topics.

Hands-on activities also include exploring the tactile senses, including Jell-O play, clay play, and bubble play.

As they move and manipulate items, children are guided through identification of shapes, colors, letters, and numbers. For instance, one activity calls for children to trace a letter found in their own name with their finger. This simple movement helps cement the letter and its sound into the child's brain.

Active waddlers benefit from guided play in a variety of activity centers, including water and sand tables, reading areas, a construction and building toys area, and an activity center used for coloring and other art projects.

At story time, teachers use props, such as puppets or the flannel board, to help bring the story to life for the child.

All care routines are created with the waddler in mind. While some children nap, others are guided through sensory experiences by a caregiver, such as touching various play objects to become familiar with a variety of textures.

Waddlers' teachers and caregivers use clean up time as an opportunity to reinforce healthy personal hygiene habits. Since children at this age love to mimic the adults around them, it is a wonderful time to teach them to wash their own hands. In addition, clean up time is an opportunity to teach the importance of putting away toys and other objects, such as manipulatives. And, as in many other phases of the day, a clean up song helps internalize and reinforce the learning.

Chapter 11

The Toddler Program (Ages 24 Months to 36 Months)

A toddler program needs to be more complex and structured than an infant or waddler program. Toddlers wake up each morning ready to tackle the world on their own; their focus is on activity and autonomy. A quality child care program must keep pace with a toddler's need to widen her world through healthy exploration and a stimulating environment.

Curriculum for Toddlers

Opportunities abound for intellectual, physical, emotional, and social development as toddlers in The Visone Method's program put their tiny feet squarely on a solid path of learning.

1. **Social and Emotional Development**
   o Toddlers learn to control themselves through self-discipline and the establishment of simple routines.
   o Teachers give praise, as toddlers become responsive to it during this stage.
   o Toddlers begin to care for themselves (under the watchful eye of a teacher) by learning how to wash their hands properly, eating an entire meal using a spoon, and trying to use a fork.
   o This is the stage where children start to transition to the potty and learn to be sensitive to their own bodies' clues that precede the need to use the potty.

2. **Language Development**
   o Toddlers are encouraged to share their experiences through verbal communication.

o Teachers talk more extensively to the toddlers while teaching new songs and poems.

o By participating in role-play and pretend games, toddlers increase their vocabulary and express themselves creatively.

o Toddlers expand upon their ability to name objects, shapes, animals, and family members.

o They begin participating in nursery rhymes.

o Toddlers are able to communicate more clearly now, using word combinations and two-and three-word sentences. They also start being able to say their own complete name.

o Toddlers start to understand when to use the word "no" appropriately and how to use pronouns such as you, me, and mine.

3. **Cognitive Development**

o Deeper discovery now takes place. Teachers reinforce recognition of objects, people, animals, letters, colors, and shapes.

o Toddlers begin to participate in discussions about the seasons, weather, holidays, and other themes.

o Manipulatives are used to develop an expanding understanding of, and interest in, math. Simple concepts in math (like sorting and matching) are reinforced.

o Toddlers are encouraged to line up blocks to make a train, imitate words, play Simon Says, pretend to cook dinner, and learn to compare large and small objects.

o When handed a photo upside down, a toddler learns to turn the photo to the correct position.

o When asked to select an eating tool from a lineup of implements including a ball, book, and spoon, the toddler understands and picks out the spoon.

4. **Motor Skill Development**

- o Toddlers are given a place to experience jumping, crawling, rolling, running, climbing, drawing, and picking things up.
- o Teachers offer games that demonstrate up, down, in and out.
- o To develop fine motor skills so necessary for writing, toddlers string beads or other objects (such as pasta shells).
- o A wide range of art materials are kept on hand to be explored.
- o Teachers work with toddlers to help them perform activities that allow them to use their hands independently, such as tearing paper, using a glue stick, or working with a pair of toddler-appropriate scissors.
- o A toddler will learn how to stack as many as eight objects.
- o Toddlers begin to finger paint.
- o Children at this age kick balls while alternating legs, march and crawl around the room, stretch muscles, hop briefly on one foot, jump on two feet, and catch a ball rolled to them and then roll it back.

What the Toddler's Day Looks Like Using The Visone Method

A toddler's day is a very busy one! Raring to get started, toddlers arrive at preschool and hit the ground running—literally.

Welcome time gives the children plenty of opportunity to dig into toys and activity centers, which are constantly reviewed and updated: puzzles, costumes, writing implements, water and sand tables, painting supplies and easels, building toys, transportation toys, art, and currently themed projects.

At circle time, a cheerful welcoming song acknowledges each child. After attendance is taken, toddlers examine their world through discovering more in-depth information about the calendar and weather, as well as the day's project theme.

Outdoor play gives young adventurers a chance to run, jump, enjoy the fresh air, observe the sky and trees, as teachers observe and guide them in gross motor skill development. Muscle stretching includes walking on tiptoes, leg raises, arm stretches, and marching. Clever ways to exercise gross motor skills include playing with balls of various sizes and textures, mazes, and footstep strips. Outdoor play not only emphasizes gross motor skills, but increases socialization skills, such as sharing and taking turns.

Music and movement focus on gross motor skills through dance. Active toddlers love this! Musical themes and instruments (maracas and tambourines, for example) are coordinated with the current weekly theme. Dancing with streamers and tracing footstep strips teach toddlers to add various elements to their movement.

Tabletime activities promote learning games that stress fine motor skills, such as working with color-form boards, beading, making shapes, and doing puzzles.

Visone Method teachers understand that puppets are a wonderful teaching and learning tool. They help create a variety of situations children can expand upon by using their own fertile, inventive imaginations. Teachers elicit creative stories and ideas from their little students. "Ready to play" give-and-take games, such as hide and seek, copycat games, or simple one-step requests aid in identifying and exploring the child's surroundings.

Story time offers a multitude of benefits, including opening toddlers' minds to the concept that the printed word has meaning.

Time for parallel, cooperative, and solitary play is also built into the schedule. Parallel play involves two children playing together or side-by-side for companionship. Cooperative play involves two or more children working together to play a game such as "house." Solitary play, of course, is doing something alone.

Clean up time now includes guidance on putting toys away, just as going outside for playtime allows the opportunity to learn how to properly put on coats on their own.

Toddlers are in transition between diapers and potty learning; The Visone Method calls for caregivers to help those children who are in this transition stage.

As in all programs, toddlers go home with a daily report showing positive milestones ("I was a great listener/helper/friend today," or "I slept __ hours today," or "I learned a new song today.").

Chapter 12

How The Visone Method Addresses Common "Early Years" Issues

Separation Anxiety—Yours and Theirs

One of the most difficult times for parents of very young children is when they have to separate from their precious little ones for the day. This can also be a stressful time for the little child who is not used to being away from his parents and has yet to learn that the separation is temporary, that parents leave but also come back.

It is common for children to be clingy when being left in a new situation, such as the first few days at an early childhood education facility. The Visone Method recognizes that this situation occurs more frequently than not and works to make the leave-taking as smooth as possible.

Prior to the first day a child starts their early childhood education program, we recommend these proven strategies to parents:

- Visit the school several times in advance, so the child can begin the transition process—becoming familiar with the school, the classroom, the teacher and caregiver, and some of the routines.

- Ask a librarian to recommend books to read together about child care and/or preschool.

- Inquire about getting names of other children in the school so that you may arrange a play-date prior to the start of school.

- A detailed personal information form should be filled out about each child for the teacher to have on file. This puts parents' minds at ease, knowing that caregivers and teachers are aware of each child's nuances. The personal information forms at HAFHA ask about each child's nap and nighttime sleep routines; what frightens each child as well as what comforts him; how the child reacts to strangers; how many ounces each child drinks each day; and the preferred foods; toys, and activities.

Once your little one begins attending the early childhood education program, the following recommendations have proven effective:

- Before coming to school, make sure there is enough time for children to eat breakfast, get dressed, and say good-bye to their favorite toys and books at home.

- Let the child bring in a comforting security object, such as a blankie or doll for naptime.

- Don't force the child into the center of the action. Many children (as well as adults) feel most comfortable if they can stand on the outside of the activity observing for a while.

- Children should not be forced to create something at their school for the purpose of bringing something home to show off to their parents.

- Most important, let the children see that their parents are happy about where their children will be spending the day.

- At pick-up time, parents should show excitement about news of the day's activities.

An experienced teacher or caregiver should spend extra time with the child who may need it. Comforting children who need extra time to adjust to their new circumstances should be second nature to the teacher in a room filled with the very youngest of children.

Teachers and other staff should also be willing to work with the parents to make sure everyone is working toward the same goal of making the child (and therefore the parent) feel secure and optimistic at drop-off time.

Biting

As each child develops in his or her own way, special concerns may arise, especially when dealing with the littlest babies and very young waddlers and toddlers.

One of the most common concerns is the issue of biting. In our experience, it is the number one concern of parents of young children. It is so prevalent that we issued a Home Away From Home Academy policy and procedure bulletin for parents and teachers to spell out how the problem should be handled.

In order to control and stop biting, we first need to determine *why* a child is biting. As stated above, biting is common among young children, but understanding why children bite is a whole other story. Children bite for different reasons under different circumstances.

Understanding the reason for the biting is the first step to changing the behavior. Use the **"Who, What, Where, When, and How" Method** to pinpoint the problem:

- Who was involved?
- What happened before or after?
- Where did it happen?
- When did the biting occur?
- How was the situation handled?

Once you ask these questions, you're likely to find that the cause falls under one of the following **Common Reasons Children Bite:**

- **Exploration:** Infants and toddlers learn by touching, smelling, hearing, and tasting. If an infant is given an object, it is likely that the infant puts it in her mouth. Tasting or "mouthing" things is something that all children do. Children at this age do not always understand the differences between gnawing on an object and biting a person.

- **Teething:** Children generally begin teething between the ages of four and seven months. Swollen, tender gums can cause a great deal of discomfort. Infants can sometimes find relief from this discomfort and pain by chewing on something. Sometimes the "object" can be a person. Again, at this age a child may not understand the difference between chewing on a toy and biting a person.

- **Cause and Effect:** At about the age of twelve months, infants become interested in finding out what happens when they do something. When they bang a spoon on the table, they discover that it makes a loud sound. When they drop their bottle from the crib, they discover it falls. They also may discover that when they bite someone, they hear a loud scream of protest.

- **Attention:** Older toddlers may bite to get attention. When children are in situations in which they are not receiving enough positive attention and daily interaction, they often find a way to make everyone sit up and notice. Being ignored is not fun. Biting is a quick way to become the center of attention, even if it attracts negative attention. In many instances, ignoring the child who bit and giving all the attention to the child who has been bitten can stop this behavior.

- **Imitation:** Older toddlers love to imitate others and find imitation to be a powerful way to learn new things. Sometimes toddlers see others bite and decide to try it themselves. When an adult bites a child back in punishment, it does not stop the biting, but rather teaches the child that biting is an acceptable form of behavior. Affectionate, playful biting by adults may send mixed signals to a child.

- **Independence:** Toddlers are trying hard to be independent. "Mine" and "Me do it" are favorite phrases. Learning to do things without help, making their own choices, and needing control over situations are all part of growing up. Biting is a powerful way to control others. If a child wants a toy or wants a playmate to leave him alone or move out of his way, biting helps him get what he wants fast.

- **Frustration:** Biting often occurs because a child is frustrated and does not know what else to do. For example, an activity may be too difficult for the child. Or there may be too many children for the child to deal with. Or the child may be angry because someone tried to take his toy away. Because the child has not yet learned the appropriate word or actions to express his frustration, he resorts to biting.

It's important to remember that young children often experience frustration. Growing up is a real struggle. Drinking from a cup is fine, but nursing or sucking from a bottle may still seem wonderful. Sometimes it would be nice to remain a baby, and leaving baby behaviors behind may trigger an inner conflict.

Keep in mind that toddlers are entering the beginning stages of language (they have trouble asking for things or requesting help) and the beginning stages of cooperative play. When a child doesn't have words to express her feelings, sometimes the child will express her feelings inappropriately by hitting, pushing, or biting.

- **Stress:** A child's world can be stressful at times. A lack of daily routine, interesting things to do, or adult interaction can create stressful situations for children. Events like death, divorce, moving to a new home, or the birth of a new baby also cause stress for children. Biting is one way to express feelings and relieve tension, since toddlers don't have the skills to negotiate or understand another person's point of view.

Once you discover a child's reason for biting, you can adopt several approaches to prevention. The following are **Recommended Strategies for Dealing with *Specific* Causes of Biting:**

- **If you determine the biting occurs as the result of exploration or teething:** You may want to provide the child with a cloth, teething ring, or other safe item to gnaw on. Don't let children see that you think biting is funny or a game. Remove the child from the situation and always say, "*No!* Biting hurts!"

- **If a child seems to bite when tired or hungry:** You many want to assess the daily routine to be sure that the child is getting enough sleep and nourishment.

- **If a child bites due to a feeling of being powerless:** The first step is to try to make sure that the child's needs are protected or to prevent her from biting. Make sure she is not getting the worst of the deal.

- **If attention-seeking seems to be the main cause for biting:** The Visone Method recommends spending more quality or positive time with the child. Give the child many opportunities for discovery and for interesting play. Read books together and play, play, play with your child. While you play, you will discover many teachable moments, model positive resolutions to situations, and build lasting memories.

- **If a child is experiencing a stressful life event that is causing biting**: Make daily life as supportive and normal as possible. Predictable meals and bedtimes, as well as extra time with a loving adult, can help. Establish consistency with daily activities, including attending school programs or specialty classes. Some activities can actually relieve tension, including rolling, squishing, and pounding play dough at school, or relaxing and splashing in the bathtub at home. In painful situations like divorce or death, time and patience are crucial for healing to occur throughout a family.

The following are **General Strategies for Handling the Issue of Biting:**

- When a child bites, show the child with voice and facial expression that biting is unacceptable. Speak firmly and look into the child's eyes. For example, you might say, "*No!* Sara, it's not okay to bite. It hurts John when you bite him. He's crying. I won't let you bite John or another child."

- If the child is able to talk, you might also say, "Use your words; tell John you need him to move instead of biting him." Give the child the words: "Say, 'Please move, John!'"

- When possible, allow the child to be part of the comforting process, as it is a good way to teach nurturing behaviors.

- Plan ahead, if possible, to avoid situations where you know the child might bite.

- Respond promptly, firmly, and calmly to biting.

- Remove the child from the situation and help him find another outlet for his feelings.

- Don't bite back. This is terrifying for the child and teaches the very thing you don't want him to learn.

- Give the child positive attention every day to build his self-esteem.

Biting is serious and is upsetting for everyone: the injured child and her parents, the parents of the biter, and the biter herself. Policies, such as the one we created at HAFHA, help determine when biting has gotten out of control. **HAFHA'S Policies and Procedures for Biting** include the following:

- Cold compresses to the wound are the first course of action to be taken, in addition, of course, to comforting the child who has been bitten. If the skin is broken, the wound is washed with soap and water immediately.

- An accident report is written and the parents called if warranted. When possible, a nurse examines the wound. The school's director is informed of the situation so an assessment can be made should this become a recurring event.

- The child who bites is removed from the area and disapproval is conveyed by the teacher's words and facial expressions. The child might be "shadowed" by caregivers to watch for any ongoing problems. Incidents are recorded and tracked so caregivers can see if patterns or reasons for the problem appear.

- The Visone Method believes that the names of the child receiving the bites and the biter should not be revealed, even to the other parents involved in the incident. If there is a health concern, the head teacher or staff nurse will gather anonymous information to give the parents of the injured child.

- If other instances of biting occur, we follow up with the biter's family to help resolve the problem. If the problem is serious and ongoing (perhaps a child bites several times a day for more than a week), we will suggest that the child be kept home from school for a while.

- The biter's family might be asked if this problem also exists at home and what action has been taken. For instance, has the pediatrician been consulted?

- If a third meeting with the biter's family is necessary, we then request that the biter be removed from the school until the situation is completely resolved.

- During the entire process, we offer suggestions and advice, as well as resources and reading material.

Biting is a difficult and uncomfortable issue for parents to deal with. If your child is the victim, you may feel angry or outraged. If your child is the biter, you may feel embarrassed and frustrated. Take heart! Most toddlers who bite do so only for a short while. Paying close attention to the circumstances will help you develop some useful solutions. Soon your toddler will have learned important new skills for communicating and getting along, especially if he or she is surrounded by caring and educated professionals in a positive school atmosphere, as well as a loving and patient family.

Chapter 13

Assessment and Observation

In addition to the important work of balancing the optimal level of stimulation with focused nurturing, The Visone Method calls for ongoing and frequent observation and assessment of each child.

Regular observations of very young children can detect speech and language delays. In addition, these observations can also help to identify forms of autism and emotional, physical, and developmental delays in time to seek professional intervention, as necessary.

For each program, we have compiled a very detailed assessment to track each child during the school career. Assessments are rated as follows: "Assistance Needed," "Progressing Toward," or "Mastered Skill."

Developmental Criteria for Ages 3 to 11 Months

Developmental criteria for a 3-month-old include:

- Looks at own fingers
- Sucks thumb
- Holds head erect in a sitting position
- Turns head toward sounds

Criteria for a 4-month-old include:

- Turns from back to side
- Can focus on objects at a distance
- "Helps" while being pulled to a sitting position

Criteria for a 5-month-old include:

- Rolls from back to stomach
- Picks up spoon

- Smiles at image in mirror
- Makes a variety of sounds: b, m, d, l, n, ah, ee, oo

Criteria for a 6-month-old include:
- Lifts head while lying on back
- Grasps tiny object between thumb and opposing fingers
- Imitates sounds made by parents and caregivers

Criteria for a 7-month-old include:
- Rocks on hands and knees
- Uses fingers to grasp finger foods
- Responds to own name
- Smiles at own image in a mirror

Criteria for an 8-month-old include:
- Pulls self to sitting position
- Bites and chews
- Enjoys listening to talk, songs, rhyming
- Babbles in sentence-like structure

Criteria for a 9-month-old include:
- Sits without support
- Investigates contents of containers by putting objects in, pouring objects out
- Responds to "no" and single directions

Criteria for a 10-month-old include:
- Sits, stands, turns, changes position, crawls
- Uses an extended finger to explore and poke small objects
- Points to simple body parts (e.g., nose, eyes, mouth)

Criteria for an 11-month-old include:

- Attempts to take a step without support
- Attempts to roll or throw a ball back and forth to caregiver
- Begins to turn pages of a book

Developmental Criteria for Ages 12 to 18 Months

A child between 12 and 18 months is assessed on forty-eight points, such as:

- Moves around the room
- Rolls a ball
- Enjoys books
- Points at or names familiar objects
- Tries to kick a ball
- Matches toys
- Shows a variety of emotions
- Chews food well
- Points to five body parts
- Says two-word sentences
- Recognizes self in photos
- Tries to comfort others

Developmental Criteria for Waddlers

At 16 months, criteria include:

- Imitates actions on toys
- Shakes head side to side to represent "no"
- Pulls off hat, socks, mittens on request
- Walks by him/herself
- Talks in nonsense sentences using speech-like patterns

- Places one object on another
- Offers something to adult and won't let go of it
- Begins to chew well

Between 16 and 19 months, criteria include:
- Can do a one-to-three-piece puzzle by him/herself
- Can express sounds animals make
- Will point to at least five body parts when named
- Will imitate stroking on paper with a crayon
- Can turn one page at a time
- Can turn over a container to remove an object inside
- Communicates needs by using single words
- Wipes and dries hands with help

Between 20 and 24 months, criteria include:
- Can take apart and put together simple objects
- Sings some words to a song
- Jumps in place
- Attempts to put shoes on
- Places three shapes (round, square, triangle) correctly on form board
- Imitates vertical and circular scribbles
- Strings large beads or manipulates other objects
- Uses action words to describe activities in pictures

Developmental Criteria for Toddlers

Emotional well-being criteria include:
- Seems secure in both active and quiet activities
- Develops the ability to share and take turns

- Identifies own gender and describes what he or she looks like
- Begins to develop ability to wait for turn and share
- Develops the ability to sit in a group to listen to a story for ten to fifteen minutes
- Expanding self-help skills include cleaning up, fetching jacket, feeding self, indicating toilet needs

Physical mastery/gross motor skills development criteria include:
- Jumps with two feet
- Hops briefly on one foot
- Tosses a ball two feet away
- Catches a rolled ball and rolls it forward
- Coordinates a series of physical skills, such as marching with alternating legs
- Vigorously pursues tumbling, crawling, and rolling with success

Perception/fine motor skills development criteria include:
- Differentiates between a circle and a square
- Draws faces (no arms or legs yet)
- Fills and dumps containers
- Develops some small muscle hand-eye coordination (e.g., manipulation of simple form boards)
- Creative art work includes gluing and pasting objects, painting with a large brush

Social interaction development criteria include:
- Prefers to play near, but not always with, other children (associative play)
- Imitates play of other children or adults
- Begins to form friendships

- Shows adaptation to and interest in surroundings
- Independently chooses a toy, activity, or play area
- Shares toys or other items with a friendly attitude
- Follows simple rules in games directed by adults
- Participates in nursery rhymes and songs with simple movements, facial expressions, and/or hand movements

Language/communication development criteria include:
- Verbalizes wants
- Verbalizes difference between "big" and "little"
- Begins to talk about meaningful experiences
- Describes situations using two or three words
- Knows first and last name between thirty months to three years
- Shows understanding of the word "not," as in "an orange, not an apple"
- Names several pictures, objects, shapes, animals, and family members

Cognitive development criteria include:
- Matches two objects of the same color
- Understands concept of "one"
- Identifies objects by their function (warm hands/mittens)
- Begins to place large puzzle pieces in the correct place

Sensory integration development criteria include:
- Can discriminate among smells (orange slices, pineapple chunks, banana)
- Finger paints with textured materials
- Identifies textures such as smooth, rough, hard, soft, etc.
- Discriminates between wet and dry

- Becomes aware of environment and weather variations

Self-care development criteria include:
- Begins to use fork
- Can unbutton, unsnap, undo a lace, and unzip
- Uses a spoon without spilling
- Begins toilet training and uses words to indicate the need to use the toilet
- Infrequent bowel accidents; remains dry between trips to toilet
- Puts on some clothes without assistance: hat, pants, pull-on shoes

Positive Transition to Next Programs

The Visone Method keeps records of all developmental observations and assessments that carry through to the next program in which the child will be enrolled.

Transitions to the next stage of the school's program should not be based on age alone. Decisions must be based on a portfolio of social, emotional, intellectual, physical, and self-help skills and include input from the child's teachers and caregivers. Only a thorough evaluation of each child's unique development can determine if, and when, a child is ready to make a transition.

PART IV

THE VISONE METHOD IN ACTION: PRESCHOOL THROUGH SECOND GRADE

Chapter 14
Growing Curious Minds—An Overview

"Education is a tree that will bear fruit."—*Rose Kennedy*

Having grown by leaps and bounds throughout their earliest years, children take a giant leap onto a new plateau when they attend preschool through second grade. They explore the world, aided by additional tools, curiosity, skills, and—of significant importance to The Visone Method—gentle, informed guidance.

Development at these stages is rapid. Your precious little bundle, who not so long ago took his first steps, as a preschooler comes home able to spell his name and accurately state his address and telephone number.

The Visone Method program for preschoolers through second-graders is more developed, structured, and academically oriented than programs for younger children. These programs immerse children more deeply into music, technology, science, and language in direct proportion to their newly expanded abilities to retain, understand, and focus on increasingly sophisticated concepts. This approach allows young ones to open themselves to more knowledge and learning.

The challenge is to stimulate and help realize students' fullest potential, and The Visone Method teachers are ready. They incorporate increased structure into their daily routines to meet developmental guidelines and enrich eager minds. The Visone Method teachers understand they are the catalyst through which their students can discover, explore, question, and problem-solve.

The Visone Method teaches preschoolers through second-graders how to learn both academic and social lessons, lessons children take with them and build upon during their entire school career. Children should be given ample opportunity to be successful in social situations during these stages. They also need to acquire the tools needed to be good citizens, to learn to accept the diversity of different cultures and customs and respect all people.

Our philosophy is that you cannot teach a child how to learn in the fourth, fifth, or sixth grades; learning to learn needs to happen during preschool through second grade. It is the time to lay the foundation for education and development, the time to open minds to as many avenues as possible. The study habits and work skills that are developed during these stages remain for a lifetime.

The following is an overview of what is taught during this important time:

- **Preschool:** Children learn the alphabet, numbers, and colors. They become familiar with personal information, such as telephone numbers, their address, and the spelling of their own name.

- **Pre-Kindergarten:** The Visone Method pre-kindergarten program advances children to a level equivalent to most public school kindergarten programs. During pre-kindergarten, children are introduced to formal writing and literature programs. Children in The Visone Method pre-kindergarten program are given every opportunity to become early readers by learning phonics and rhyming. Likewise, they are taught beginning addition and subtraction concepts.

- **Kindergarten:** As children enter kindergarten, they are ready for more structure in their program. Eager to learn and so excited about "being big," they are ready to work in books and begin their "real" school life. By December of the kindergarten year, it all falls into place, and children are reading. By the end of kindergarten, their reading jumps to second-grade level.

Chapter 15

I'm a Big Kid Now—Preschool and Pre-Kindergarten

Preschool

Preschoolers (children three to four years old) are ready for a wider world to explore, and they have many new abilities they are ready to test. Their imaginations are catching up with their skills. Always on the go, they learn by doing. What better way to find out how a caterpillar becomes a butterfly than to observe one personally? Preschoolers are themselves like the butterflies: transforming, as we watch, into children with ever increasing social, intellectual, and physical talents.

The Visone Method preschool meets the challenge of keeping its students interested, while nurturing not only a love of learning, but the children's self-esteem. Guiding a preschooler through activities such as beginning reading or reading readiness, opening the window wider on math and science concepts, or introducing the skill of strategizing encourages the growing, curious mind of a preschooler who is taking tenuous steps toward independence.

Developmental Factors The Visone Method Preschool Considers

1. **Social and Emotional Development**
   o Preschoolers are learning to share toys, express feelings, and cooperate in groups.
   o Preschoolers are proud that they are ready to learn self-reliance, self-control, and independence.
   o At this age, children start looking forward to spending time with other children.
   o At this age, children begin to realize there is give-and-take when they play with others.

o Preschoolers begin to understand that people have similarities as well as differences.

2. **Language Development**

o Preschoolers are eager to increase their vocabulary.

o Preschoolers begin using more descriptive words and listen more carefully for new ways to communicate.

o Teachers further language skills by guiding preschoolers through more sophisticated books, computer projects, and opportunities for interaction with others.

o Teachers help develop preschoolers' listening skills by telling stories. (Listening skills come before reading skills.)

o Preschoolers are ready to learn the proper names for articles of clothing and the proper uses of *I, me,* and *you.*

3. **Cognitive Development**

o Preschoolers are able to recognize and remember more.

o They're ready to use manipulatives to learn math concepts, and they're ready to understand new media and technology.

o Preschoolers are ready to learn new practical skills, such as taking on and off their coats.

o Preschoolers are ready to learn proper health regimes.

o Preschoolers are ready to learn how to identify what's missing from a picture, recognize pair-related items (such as shoes and socks), and draw stick figures.

4. **Motor Skill Development**

o Preschoolers need plenty of opportunities to run, jump, and climb.

o Preschoolers need to continue developing their fine motor skills, so necessary for beginning writing proficiencies. The Visone Method calls for many hand-eye coordination activities to foster fine motor skills.

o Preschoolers should learn to throw a ball overhand and roll a large ball to a target in the distance.

Preschool Curriculum

A preschooler is busy from the moment he arrives at school, and his education should be a balance between independent discovery and hands-on guidance. Each area of the curriculum should play off another so that learning is seamless and integrated—and fun! Computer games teach math and reading skills; music reinforces learning the alphabet; and planning for a special event develops social skills.

1. **Reading and Language Arts**

   o At HAFHA, two new letters of the alphabet are discussed each month.

   o Preschoolers learn about lowercase letters.

   o A preschooler learns to recognize letters in her name and how to put the letters together to form her name.

   o Phonics is introduced, strengthening each child's early reading readiness.

2. **Music**

   o Preschoolers learn that appreciating music is as important as learning the words to songs or the hand movements that go along with them.

   o Preschoolers play appropriate child-sized instruments and listen to a variety of music genres.

   o Preschoolers have several opportunities to show off their performing talents. This helps build self-esteem, poise, and confidence.

   o Music is integrated as a tool into all of the preschooler's lessons.

3. **Science**

   o Preschoolers learn to improve their observation skills.

   o They learn how and why things work.

o Each month, preschoolers explore a different theme, from the five senses to plant life.

o A credentialed science teacher conducts fun experiments with the preschoolers.

4. **Math**

o Preschoolers learn the numerical concepts between one and twenty. Basic, easy-to-grasp visuals of these numbers are illustrated through math studies and everyday, real-world activities.

5. **Library**

o Teachers read to the preschoolers every day.

o Preschoolers have the opportunity to "read" to each other by describing the action in the illustrations.

o Preschoolers learn basic library skills and the conventions of reading.

6. **Social Studies**

o Preschoolers learn about other cultures. They are exposed to maps, globes, and books that demonstrate cultural differences. This helps build goodwill and self-esteem for all students, while also teaching about tolerance.

o Preschoolers learn about different careers, how the preschoolers can fit into their community, and how the preschoolers can support and enhance their community.

7. **Art**

o Teachers provide preschoolers with a variety of art materials and guide the children as they experiment in a nurturing setting.

o Teachers give preschoolers the freedom to try lots of techniques without criticism that hinders that freedom.

o Preschoolers draw and paint with different sized art tools, fostering hand-eye coordination and fine motor skills as the children expresses themselves with color.

8. **Computers**

- o Preschoolers have computers in their classroom. An early foray into the world of technology gives children the foundation and confidence they need to grow in this area.

- o Preschoolers learn how a computer works and how to take care of it.

- o Teachers provide a plethora of preschool-friendly interactive programs and CD ROMs that the children can use.

Pre-Kindergarten

Visone Method teachers guide their pre-kindergarteners (ages four to five years old) into a curriculum that puts them ahead of other pre-kindergarteners. Our research has led us to understand what educational opportunities should be instituted within an environment of nurtured social growth and interaction. Balance between these factors is the foundation of our goals.

Pre-kindergarten is one of the most critical times in a child's life for literacy development. Pre-kindergarteners are ready to learn a second language while, emotionally, they are developing into totally social beings who must make clear decisions about what they like and don't like. Music and movement play even more important roles at this stage.

Advancements in all areas of learning—from computers to reading to music and math—are now within grasp of the budding pre-kindergartener. The Visone Method teacher is on hand to make sure the children can easily reach toward new levels as they become inspired and excited about learning.

The pre-kindergarten classroom at HAFHA is divided into learning zones, each equipped with the best tools available for that particular area of learning. The zones have defined boundaries so that children may better understand the rules and tools of each area, as well as learn the disciplines needed (with the guidance of their teachers, of course) in each of the learning areas. After they complete an activity in one zone and clean up after themselves, the children are able to flow easily to another learning zone.

A good pre-kindergarten classroom designed with centers promotes learning in all developmental and academic areas. The concepts learned in these centers cross over into many areas of learning. Learning games can promote academic awareness in math, science, social studies, and language arts—while building fine motor skills. Two children building a tower together in the block area not only learn spatial concepts, but build social skills as well. If the children are pretending with dinosaurs, they are learning new words, such as "extinct" or "reptiles." When playing with "career people," they experience varied walks of life as they play.

Learning games are an integral part of The Visone Method's pre-kindergarten classroom as well. In the areas of math, science, and language arts, games increase and reinforce multiple skills. Lacing and stringing different-sized beads reinforces hand-eye coordination and fine motor skills. Practice with fun patterning games, number games, and measurement tools helps build beginning math basics. Opposite cards help reinforce important skills in language arts.

Science games can reinforce the five senses. Children are allowed to explore with magnets and magnifying glasses and are given the words to describe textures as they explore. They simultaneously learn the composition and uses of those objects.

Other games, such as counting how many green bears can fill a green cup or how many blue bears will balance the scale, stimulate critical thinking and reasoning abilities. Math manipulatives reinforce lessons about shapes, sizes, and patterns.

As children pretend in a dramatic play or kitchen area, they act out emotions while they solve day-to-day problems. A good Visone Method teacher learns a great deal about a child by observing how the child interacts with dolls and the other children in the housekeeping areas.

The pre-kindergarten classroom is organized into well-thought-out zones, each filled with all the necessary tools, equipment, and materials. As children observe, explore, and learn, they develop and enrich their curious minds.

Pre-Kindergarten Curriculum

Much thought and research has gone into the pre-kindergarten curriculum we produce at HAFHA. We consider all pre-kindergarteners' needs to ensure the opportunity exists to realize their utmost potential.

1. **Reading and Language Arts**

    o   Pre-kindergarteners identify uppercase and lowercase letters, while reinforcing the sounds each letter makes. They also practice writing both uppercase and lowercase letters.

    o   Pre-kindergarteners learn the alphabet.

    o   A Writing Table in the classroom allows the pre-kindergartener to put his fine motor skills to work.

    o   Pre-kindergarteners learn refined writing techniques, such as how to hold a pencil correctly.

2. **Music**

    o   Pre-kindergarteners learn about different composers and their respective music styles and techniques.

    o   They are encouraged to "compose" on appropriately sized keyboards—exploring with sounds, tempos, and beats.

    o   A credentialed music teacher introduces instrument categories, scales, and lessons to teach pre-kindergarteners to decipher the different sounds of each instrument.

    o   Pre-kindergarteners develop listening skills as they explore questions such as "Is it an opera or show tune we are listening to?"

    o   Harmonies and counterpart singing is taught using fun, catchy, silly songs—and the children sing their hearts out. Self-esteem rises as friendly audience members of the class applaud for each other. Applause is the best medicine for a sad or shy beginning music-maker or a budding actor.

3. **Science**

   o Pre-kindergarteners focus on life, physical, and environmental sciences.

   o Science-related objects (e.g., magnets, rocks, and shells) are available for children to observe in classroom centers. Such objects spark curiosity as scientific principles are introduced.

4. **Math**

   o Pre-kindergarteners learn about numbers, adding, subtracting, and measuring.

   o They learn about shapes, sizes, and patterns.

   o Children learn mathematical concepts, social skills, and hand-eye coordination by playing with blocks.

5. **Library**

   o With many excellent books to choose from in a well-stocked pre-kindergarten library, children are free to make choices.

   o Teachers expose children to the wonder of libraries in order to ensure a love of reading throughout their lives.

6. **Social Studies**

   o Teachers stress an understanding of the child's environments at home, at school, and in the community.

7. **Art**

   o Pre-kindergarteners learn simple science by mixing colors.

   o They promote their fine motor skills by using colorful modeling clay.

   o They improve hand-eye coordination and fine motor development by shading and tracing.

   o When a child is cutting from magazines, he builds strength in his fingers as well as learns to make decisions: "What pictures do I like?" (While deciding what we like may sound like a simple chore, decision-making can be a challenge for some adults, as well as small children.)

o   Teachers often play music while the children draw; their illustrations reflect not only their creativity, but a variety of moods and feelings inspired by the music.

8.   **Dramatic Play**

o   By donning different costumes and handling different props, children enjoy the opportunity to assume different roles and interact with others in their new personas.

o   Great teachable moments arise as teachers encourage the pre-kindergarteners to expand their thinking through their new roles.

9.   **Computers**

o   Lessons include the proper way to operate computers and instruction about the computer's components, keyboard, and software.

o   Programs used are all learning-based, reinforcing math, language arts, science, art, and other subjects.

Out of the Mouths of Babes

Before we continue outlining our documented curricula, it's important to take a short intermission and look at the lighter side of the young minds that we so caringly teach. Children are a precious gift, and they speak their minds while allowing you to see their hearts. Every child makes an impact on a teacher's life; these adorable little people sometimes say the funniest things. It's important to remember their innocence and sweetness.

Written by a toddler's teacher:

•   In December, when we were getting ready for our Holiday Show, we sang lots of special songs, including "Oh Hanukkah." A little girl in our class sang her heart out, so we asked her to come to the front of the class and show her friends how the song goes. She sang like this ... "Oh Monica, Oh Monica!"

Quotes from young preschoolers:

- As a child was creating in the art area, he was heard saying to a friend, "I'm working on my masterpiece!"

- "This is the best day I ever had in my whole life," a child shouted after a birthday was celebrated in class.

- "OK, I'm putting my voice on," a child stated when a teacher asked him to please say "Good morning."

- When the children were learning about people from around the world and the fact that we all have our own special heritage, one child said "My mommy is from Ireland, my daddy is from England, and I'm from this land is your land!"

Treasured moments from pre-kindergarteners:

- A little boy said, "My mommy told me that she loves me with all her heart—with all her soul—and more than life!"

- "That movie isn't a rated R movie, it's a DVD!"

- A little boy said to his teacher, "You are 100 percent woman!"

- A child was upset in the bathroom, as he needed to change his clothing. He cried out, "Oh, my goodness, I don't want to borrow someone else's underwear! No, I can't … What am I going to do? … My mommy will be mad at me … Oh, no! … Oh, look … is that Spiderman undies? … OK, I'll wear them!"

- "You are the *bestest* teacher in the whole world!"

- At naptime, a child asked for a hug so he could fall asleep. The teacher had just given the child a hug. The child responded by saying, "Well, come here and give me another hug! I am the student, and I pay money!"

- During library time, a child was reading a multicultural story that had a picture of a menorah. The teacher asked the child what she was reading. Before the child had a chance to answer, another child chimed in, saying, "I know because I'm Jewish!" To which the other girl said, "Oh yeah? Well, I'm selfish!"

- At snack time, a teacher was talking to the children about their favorite foods. One child said steak, the other said chicken. The teacher said that she liked all kinds of fish. The children made funny faces, then one little girl said, "I like fish, too. My favorite fish is the pretzel ones!"

Chapter 16
Joining the Backpack Brigade—Kindergarten

Kindergarten is the start of something big, the demarcation between laying the foundation and constructing the building that will last through a lifetime.

Kindergarteners today are expected to know more than ever before, as they build upon their previous experiences and learning. The children taught under The Visone Method will continue to excel in an upward spiral as they step onto the threshold of the elementary school years. As parents and children enter into this new era of learning, there is much hope and expectation, which is fulfilled with a solid Visone Method start.

With even stronger guidance and more structured time in the classroom, children strengthen and hone their skills, welcome new ones, and jump into the day with an eagerness they've developed during their earlier learning experiences.

In an advanced program such as The Visone Method, the kindergartner's educational horizons are greatly broadened. We remain committed to discovering the developmental level and ideal learning style of each child, in order to foster social, emotional, and physical development. It is our belief that a group environment will benefit your child as she learns to work cooperatively with peers.

Kindergarten at HAFHA offers a strong skills-based, full-day curriculum that is comprehensive in all areas. A variety of tools, including CD ROMs, help children further their typing and reading skills, as well as others. Our rich program includes field trips, school performances, special guest presentations, music, physical activities, dance, and art. Each part of the kindergarten program helps to strengthen, heighten, and widen the learning experience.

Kindergarten Curriculum

1. **Reading**

   o Kindergarteners continue to enhance their reading skills, along with writing and listening.

   o The basic components of learning the English language—such as the variety of sounds letters make and how they blend to form words—are examined.

   o Books are chosen that relate reading, handwriting, listening, and oral language skills to one another.

   o Teachers read children's classics, fables, and folk and fairy tales, in order to deepen the child's connection to great literature. Great literature provides a model for great writing and builds vocabulary as rich language is absorbed.

   o Music is integrated, helping children become more proficient in reading as well as writing.

2. **Language Arts**

   o The kindergartener learns the rudiments of spelling and begins to identify words. How proud of themselves they are as the letter sounds they learn develop into words they figure out on their own!

   o Children advance to spell three-, four-, and five-letter words by learning to blend the sounds of letters. They retain their new skill with the aid of spelling tests.

   o They begin to perfect study skills that they will build on during their entire school life.

   o Each day, kindergarteners are given time to "write" in their individual journals, sharing their stories and experiences through drawings. The Visone Method teacher then helps them interpret their drawings with the proper words.

3. **Math**

o Math is everywhere! Sorting, classifying, graphing, measuring, counting, patterns, shapes (such as the rhombus, pentagon, and parallelogram), beginning fractions, beginning subtraction and addition, money, and time are some of the heady math concepts a Visone Method kindergartener learns.

o The method we use to teach math builds number-sense confidence. It is our goal to encourage children to investigate, question, reason, verify, and apply math concepts.

o Valuable techniques teach children how to identify numbers and understand the relationship between a number and a set.

o Doing activities at classroom math learning centers helps children retain their new knowledge in fun ways, such as playing with manipulatives.

4. **Science**

o The science curriculum includes life, physical, and earth sciences, investigation of body parts and their functions, the five senses, seasons, weather, and the environment.

o We employ a science teacher to conduct weekly experiments that challenge the kindergartener's mind. Science experiments that support the current theme are conducted in the classroom.

o Each of our kindergarten students works on a project that they will present (and be graded on) during the school's annual science fair.

5. **Health**

o The areas of physical health, exercise, nutrition, personal hygiene, and dealing with one's emotions—including what qualities are needed for good sportsmanship—are delved into on a deeper level than before.

o These subjects are taught under the direction of a certified nutritionist and a gym instructor.

6. **Social Studies**

   o Teachers prepare curricula that develop a more complete under-standing of the children's familiar environments—at home, school, in their community—through the study of community helpers, holidays, geography, current events, careers, famous people, and even the election process.

   o As with other subjects, children have classroom aids, such as an age-appropriate weekly newspaper that focuses on history, news-worthy events, and monthly themes.

7. **Foreign Language**

   o Children learn the basics of elementary vocabulary (numbers, days of the week, months, colors, shapes, greetings, common words, and phrases) in a second language.

8. **Music and Movement**

   o As children step up to the challenges of elementary school, music and movement retain their important roles. As we've already seen, music not only grows brain connections, but also adds to the stu-dent's understanding of math.

   o By creating and appreciating music and listening, singing, and dancing to it, kindergarteners learn about cultures from around the world.

   o Kindergarteners learn about composers from around the world, as well as conductors, musicians, and the instruments they play.

   o They are guided through the basics of composing, musical inter-pretation, rhythm, beat, pitch, timing, musical moods, and expression.

   o Kindergarteners delight in the opportunity to show off their musi-cal and performing skills in front of their families and invited guests.

9. **Physical Education**

   o Through cooperative physical play, children's large muscles grow stronger and healthier.

   o A foundation of routine exercise at this age sets the stage for the child's lifetime of fitness. With obesity such a concern in this country, getting into a fitness routine at a young age is a necessity.

   o Play also helps children develop the large muscle skills needed for team sports and other physical activities—in addition to learning to work and play cooperatively with classmates.

10. **Art**

    o Akin to music activities, art activities increase appreciation as well as skills.

    o Kindergarteners are ready to learn various art applications and the proper use and care of more "grownup" art materials.

    o The same themes that are explored through other subjects are explored through art in the kindergarten class.

    o The styles and lives of famous artists (such as Picasso, Van Gogh, and Monet) are introduced.

    o Little artists have an opportunity for their own "gallery" showing through a school-wide art show.

11. **Penmanship**

    o Having started building their fine muscle skills in earlier years, the students are ready to start refining their penmanship, writing letters in both upper and lower cases.

    o As they practice writing, they also refine their pencil-and paper-holding techniques by copying sentences that the teacher has put on the board onto lined paper. This task requires sophisticated hand-eye coordination—watching the chalkboard, keeping their place on the lined paper, and writing on the lines.

12. Computers and Technology

o As they progress through kindergarten, students will become more proficient with computers, practicing on a variety of software, as well as on the keyboard.

o It is important that they have independent time to explore, increasing their enthusiasm for and appreciation of what they can accomplish through a full understanding of the new technology.

o Teachers reinforce that computers are not toys, but tools with an enormous capacity for educating and creating. Used properly, they can draw, compose, store writing, and find answers.

o Computers help revise and construct concepts, as well as motivate and aid students to achieve.

o Sharing computer time with their classmates increases students' ability to interact socially while they become confident in their abilities.

In addition, kindergarteners have the chance to shine as the Star of the Week, allowing classmates to learn more about each other. HAFHA schools also participate in wonderful national programs, such as "Book It," in which children are given monthly reading goals. When the students meet those goals, they are rewarded with coupons for pizza. What fun!

At the end of each school day, kindergarteners take home a page or so of homework. Homework not only reinforces the learning that went on in the classroom, but also affords parents the opportunity to be more intimately involved with their child's education.

Chapter 17
First in Class—First Grade

While many early childhood education facilities end their curriculum with kindergarten, The Visone Method at HAFHA continues into the first and second grades. Because of our teaching methods and philosophies, our students far surpass their peers in public school.

As she conquers skills needed in the first grade, the child taught under The Visone Method develops a masterful grasp of concepts and academic basics and develops physically, emotionally, and socially. Small classes, by design, allow for more individual attention from knowledgeable teachers. Children are exposed to the joys of working independently toward their personal best, as well as supporting and learning from each other in a group.

The first-grader has grown so much. By this point in his education, The Visone Method has worked to help him understand his role in the community as well in the classroom. Working together on ways to help those less fortunate and to better the environment, first-graders become rooted in the world outside of themselves. Learning about other cultures allows them to see how they fit into the bigger picture.

First grade is about making learning fun, continuing with successes, and stretching possibilities. First-graders ride along on the amazing adventure that leads to knowledge.

First-Grade Curriculum

1. **Reading and Language Arts**
   o High-quality children's literature fully integrates reading and language arts for the first-grader. Subject matter encourages students to examine their own life experiences as well as a variety of genres and themes. Themes also support reading in other subject areas. With quality literature, the student develops into a fluent reader and life-

long lover of books. The positive attributes that develop from reading include proficient writing skills and an expanded vocabulary. Children also learn critical thinking and reasoning skills.

o First-grade readers advance their spelling skills as they learn about consonants, long and short vowels, and words that rhyme.

o Work in phonics is more mature, with activities that demonstrate sequentially more sophisticated levels of reading and language arts. This includes cluster words, digraphs, possessives, etc.

o A variety of assessments evaluate the child's growing reading and writing abilities.

o Study skills, along with reading for enjoyment, are stressed.

o Students participate in shared reading, as well as in sustained silent reading on their own.

2. **Writing**

o No matter what your child chooses to do with her life as an adult, good writing will be a part of it. First-graders start putting their thoughts on paper, mustering all the skills they have been taught thus far, adding to their knowledge through using proper writing conventions.

o First-graders create word lists and write daily journals.

o The mechanics of grammar support a program of learning the writing process—from pre-writing, where the student starts with thoughts or facts, to re-writing, editing, proofreading, and finally "publishing" the work on the computer, be it a poem, letter, or book report.

o A portfolio of the child's work demonstrates the progress she makes during the school year.

3. **Math**

o It is our belief that every child can be successful in the important subject of math, given the right tools and the right teaching methods. Building upon what they've already learned, our first-graders at HAFHA *reason* math solutions, as opposed to *memorizing* them. With this technique, they are able to develop higher decision-making and thinking skills.

o With more challenging problems than before, children learn several ways to figure solutions to the same problem through continued use of manipulatives.

o Some of the goals for first-graders are: learning place values up to 100; learning strategies for addition and subtraction, including two-digit numbers; learning shapes, patterns, fractions, and the rudiments of measurement.

4. **Social Studies**

o Visone Method first-graders become compassionate citizens of the world community, learning about the values and rules of many societies and cultures.

o We examine the past through history lessons and study the present by following current events.

o Focuses of study include holidays, map skills, geography, economics, famous citizens of different cultures, following timelines, and distinguishing boundaries, in neighborhoods as well as around the globe.

o Students establish pen pals domestically and internationally.

o At HAFHA, students also correspond with our sister school in Africa.

5. **Science**

o Children have a natural curiosity about the world around them. The Visone Method encourages a first-grader's natural curiosity by developing hands-on experiments that fully absorb the child's interests.

o Children hone their skills by organizing their data, as well as recording and evaluating their observations.

o The children learn to hypothesize and verify.

o A few of our scientific interests in first grade include the solar system, living versus non-living things, animals, plants, magnets, the environment, matter, and dental health.

6. **Health**

o As children grow, personal care becomes an increasingly important issue. Teaching children the facts about their bodies is crucial to a lifetime of self-respect. Topics we find important include manners, safety, exercise, proper rest, nutrition, emotions, self-esteem, and good character traits.

o Children learn that healthy bodies and healthy minds equal healthy lifestyles.

7. **Foreign Language**

o We find Spanish to be an important second language to teach young students, considering the prevalence of Spanish-speaking people in the world.

o To improve vocabulary, accent, and usage, reviews of what the students have learned so far precede new lessons. Included are words about school, family, clothing, foods, and the outdoors.

o Necessary phrases are also learned, such as, "Hello," "How are you?" and "Good-bye."

8. **Public Speaking**

o Students memorize a poem each month and recite it in front of peers at circle time.

o First-graders share experiences, pictures, stories, poems, and ideas in front of the class as they begin to lose their inhibitions about public speaking.

o Music plays a big role in public speaking, especially when children get opportunities to perform on a big stage. Music promotes confidence, poise, and proper diction—the tools necessary to become a great public speaker.

9. **Handwriting**

   o Learning to produce fluent, legible handwriting is just as important as learning the conventions of writing. Each day, students have time to practice their handwriting skills and integrate their flourishing handwriting into writing projects.

   o Writing letters, numbers, words, and sentences develops proficiency.

   o Children are taught to take pride in their neat handwriting.

10. **Computers and Technology**

    o Computers and new technologies are such a blessing for today's first-graders. They are not only fun and practical, but they open the door to a world unimaginable even a generation ago. The Visone Method teacher guides, instructs, and helps the children develop values and principles through using computers.

    o With computers, students thoroughly investigate topics and build concepts.

    o Each week, first-graders have forty-five minutes to one hour of computer instruction, with time for writing and illustrating their own stories, letters, and poems.

11. **Library**

    o With a library of excellent books in a variety of genres right in the classroom, we structure library procedures more stringently. Readers choose books according to their interest and level of ability and are then responsible for signing books in and out and returning books neatly in the right place on the shelf.

    o Readers are also encouraged to use the appropriate vocabulary, such as *author*, *illustrator*, and *subject*.

12. **Art**

    o As in the lower grades, art is woven into each day in The Visone Method first-grade program.

o Children experiment with various media and study fine art, learning about the artists who created the pieces.

o Design elements encompass color, shape, texture, form, line, and space—and include the freedom to create and have fun.

13. **Gym**

o After several hours engrossed in challenging and stimulating academics, first-graders are ready to let loose with a gym program designed to increase fine and gross motor skills: throwing and catching balls, balance skills, eye-foot coordination, and other types of movement.

o First-graders also take a look at the human skeletal structure, learning about muscles and bones.

o The values of cooperation and good sportsmanship are put to the test as sports and games are practiced.

14. **Music**

o Last but not least, first-graders sing and create songs on their own as well as with the class.

o In keeping with The Visone Method's ongoing theme of cultural awareness, children listen to music from around the world, identifying nuances along with conductors, composers, instruments, and musicians.

Chapter 18
Onward and Upward—Second Grade

With their feet firmly on the path to excellent academic careers, Visone Method second-graders round out their early childhood education with extraordinary challenges met with colossal enthusiasm.

Our skills-based curriculum in second grade broadens capabilities in all subjects and enhances students' critical thinking strategies. We build a deeper understanding of the world outside the door through celebrations, special visitors who share insights with us, and appropriate field trips.

Second-graders become more well-rounded learners by working independently, as well as at the teacher's direction, through learning centers in the classroom, and in groups.

After extensive research into second-grade curriculums offered in other schools, we compiled The Visone Method schedule of learning, which outshines any other curriculum we've seen. It exceeds accepted second-grade standards and stimulates a child's growing independence toward a lifelong love of learning.

Second-Grade Curriculum

1. **Reading and Language Arts**
   o Children continue to be exposed to the best fiction and nonfiction available and are encouraged to read more on their own, especially relative to the second-grade curriculum.
   o In addition to the literature available to the students, the second-grade program offers workbooks for spelling, phonics, language, and grammar.
   o Children are guided as they apply spelling strategies to their own writing, increasing their literacy skills.

o Children are guided to choose the right words to use in their writing and to use grammar correctly when they speak.

o Assessments include evaluations of the student's ability in the major reading skills of decoding, building vocabulary, comprehension, literary appreciation, and dictionary, study, and editing skills.

o Second-graders also take great pride in their ability to properly write a letter to someone and show off their burgeoning cursive writing skills.

2. **Math**

o Children continue to learn math through *reasoning* instead of *memorizing* rules and procedures. Math has a powerful effect on a child's ability to think critically, reason, and make decisions.

o Some of the goals for second grade include: recognizing place value up to 10,000; measurement in inches, centimeters, and kilograms; temperature; addition and subtraction of triple-digit numbers using regrouping; graphing; and multiplication and division.

3. **Social Studies**

o The study of the interdependence between the student and his social and physical environments helps build an understanding of the need for laws, equality, and justice. This year, students are ready to learn how a democratic government in the United States works to support those social needs.

o Students become well-informed, compassionate, and caring citizens through the study of past and present events that shape our history.

o Some of the topics covered include the fifty states, Native Americans, the branches of government, and pre-historic animals.

4. **Science**

o The goals of our second-grade science program include helping children understand scientific advancements, dilemmas, and ethical questions. This is an excellent opportunity for a student to make decisions based on the student's own research, coming to conclusions through understanding and logic rather than superstition or bias.

o Visone Method students are given the materials to discover scientific meaning. Our approach is three-pronged: hands-on experimentation, reading scientific textbooks, and visualizing scientific concepts.

o Some of the topics we cover include: pre-historic life; life through the ages; heat and change; light and sound; ocean life; the rain forest; machines; space; and reptiles.

5. **Health**

o As the children mature, they will face more challenges, including making choices about their health (both mental and physical) and lifestyle that will affect the rest of their lives. We focus on guiding them to make decisions based on facts, so they can weave their knowledge into their daily habits.

o Some of the topics we discuss include setting and making goals, managing stress, practicing refusal skills, and resolving conflicts.

6. **Foreign Language**

o Second-graders continue to receive instruction in the language, customs, and cultures of the Spanish-speaking citizens of the world.

o We review what we have learned so far, including days of the week, months, numbers through 100, and colors. Then the children learn additional words and phrases—how to say their names in Spanish, as well as how to use the vocabulary word of the week.

o They begin to converse in Spanish.

7. **Computers and Technology**

o Our program guides our second-graders to powerful learning experiences through computers and knowledge of technology.

o We use a beginning Spanish language-learning computer program to reinforce what the student learns during Spanish lessons.

o Students learn various computer terms and review how to operate the computer on a more sophisticated level. Our second-grade students continue to amaze us with their higher level thinking skills, developed in part through their exposure to computers.

o They become even more proficient in their keyboarding skills, as well as in using the computer to help them in other subject areas.

o Second-graders use programs that focus on spelling, phonics, reading, writing, drawing, and math.

o Teachers guide the second-graders around the Internet, where they learn to gather information.

8. **Library**

o Once a week, the second-graders are given the chance to check out two books of their choice from the classroom library. The best part is they get to take the books home for a week.

o Students continue to practice good library habits—caring for books, learning the names of parts of a book, placing books back on the shelf in alphabetical order, finding books in the library card catalog, and using call numbers to retrieve the books they want.

9. **Art**

o Throughout each day, art projects relevant to what is being taught are woven into the curriculum.

o In addition, art is practiced several times during the week with a variety of art materials, textures, colors, and methods.

o The students share their projects with each other.

o Art lessons are explored both in the class and at home.

o With their fine motor skills developing more each day, student's artwork is showing more maturity as expressed through choice of design.

o At this stage, students learn size relationship, as well as distance and space perception.

10. Gym

o We believe in providing a physically challenging gym program that stimulates the student. A variety of activities, including expanded sports programs and games, meets the physical needs of the growing second-grader.

o While physical activities are designed to develop gross and fine motor skills, there are other benefits: the student gets opportunities to work on social, intellectual, and emotional abilities as well.

o Students are guided through fun physical activities as they develop a lifelong love of exercising.

11. Music

o No well-rounded educational program would ever be complete without music. Listening, singing, moving, dancing, and expressing creativity—music brings a wealth of riches to the second-grade student.

o Learning about music from around the world reinforces other classroom lessons about international cultures and worldwide citizenry.

o Musical concepts continue to be built upon. Students also expand their knowledge about composers, instruments, and composition, including pitch, timing, and mood.

o They also learn to read music, a skill that will always serve them. Listening to quality music and learning to appreciate it continues to enrich the child's life.

Chapter 19

Assessment and Observation

Visone Method students are evaluated two (preschool through pre-kindergarten) to four (kindergarten through second grade) times per year. Parents receive report cards with detailed, specific evaluations and teacher observations. A portfolio of the child's work demonstrates their progress.

Developmental Criteria for Preschool and Pre-Kindergarteners

In preschool and pre-kindergarten, students are assessed on seventy-nine points. Following are some of those developmental criteria.

1. **In cognitive skill development, does the child:**
   o   Ask questions
   o   Show curiosity about new things
   o   Recall three objects from a group she previously saw
   o   Identify what doesn't belong in a group of three items
   o   Dramatize a simple story

2. **In language arts, does the child:**
   o   Speak in four-to six-word sentences
   o   Memorize and repeat simple prose and songs
   o   Listen to short stories and simple poems
   o   Name articles of clothing
   o   Name or recognize upper and lower case letters, the four seasons, days of the week, and months of the year

3. **In social studies, does the child:**
   o   Begin to participate in a group

4. **In math, does the child:**
   o   Tell how many objects there are in a group (up to six items)
   o   Sort objects into two categories
   o   Label shapes
   o   Construct blocks when given a model
   o   Recognize the numbers 1 through 31 on the calendar

5. **In science, does the child:**
   o   Understand there are many kinds of animals
   o   Know that animals move in different ways
   o   Understand that air is everywhere
   o   Name three primary colors

6. **In gross motor skill development, does the child:**
   o   Throw a beanbag at a target five feet away
   o   Throw a ball overhand accurately
   o   Walk forward and backward on an eight-foot line
   o   Ride a tricycle

7. **In fine motor skill development, does the child:**
   o   Make balls and snakes with clay
   o   Place pegs into pegboards
   o   Hold crayons with fingers versus fist
   o   Lace-up following a sequence of holes

Developmental Criteria for Kindergarteners

In kindergarten, students are assessed on fifty-six points. Included below are some of those developmental criteria.

Students are now graded by letter:

O = outstanding

S = satisfactory

U = unsatisfactory

I = shows improvement

N = needs improvement

1. **In reading and language arts, does the child:**
   - o Listen attentively as others speak
   - o Use age-appropriate vocabulary
   - o Comprehend what he is reading
   - o Show proficiency in spelling
   - o Recognize upper and lower case letters
   - o Know phonic sounds

2. **In math, does the child:**
   - o Recognize numbers between 0 and 20
   - o Understand time and money
   - o Understand measuring
   - o Sort by color, shape, and size
   - o Count by sets

3. **In fine motor skills, does the child:**
   - o Use scissors correctly
   - o Have adequate control of the pencil
   - o Write letters correctly
   - o Write numbers correctly

4. **In gym activities, does the child:**
   - o Demonstrate sportsmanship

o Demonstrate large muscle coordination

o Begin learning the give and take of play

5. **In creative expression, does the child:**

o Show interest in music and art

o Generate ideas in dramatic play

6. **In social and personal development, does the child:**

o Use self-control

o Contribute to group discussions

o Respect others and their property

o Complete tasks independently

o Exhibit self-confidence

7. **Does the child know "all about me":**

o Her address

o Her telephone number

o Her birthday

8. **In social studies, does the child understand:**

o Yesterday, today, and tomorrow

o The concept of friendship

o Morning and afternoon

9. **In penmanship, does the child:**

o Color within the lines

o Write his name from memory

Developmental Criteria for First-and Second-Graders

In first and second grades, children are graded in thirty-three categories. In addition to the categories listed below, students are also graded in penmanship, health, social studies, art, music, and gym.

Students are still graded by letter:

O = outstanding

S = satisfactory

U = unsatisfactory

I = shows improvement

N = needs improvement

1. **Reading Skills**
   o Comprehension
   o Oral reading
   o Phonics

2. **Language Skills**
   o Grammar use
   o Written communication
   o Oral communication
   o Spelling

3. **Math Skills**
   o Understands concepts
   o Masters whole facts and skills
   o Uses reason to solve problems

4. **Work Habits**
   o Listens attentively
   o Works neatly and with organization
   o Follows directions
   o Participates

5. **Conduct**

   o   Shows self-control

   o   Plays well with others

   o   Accepts responsibility

PART V

PULLING IT ALL TOGETHER

Chapter 20

Fifteen Critical Keys to a Successful Early Childhood Education Facility

FACT: Elementary schools today expect children to enter kindergarten with reading and math readiness skills.

FACT: According to research by many organizations, including the Child Trauma Academy, 90 percent of a child's brain is developed by age five.

FACT: The National Association for the Education of Young Children found the traditional approach to curriculum (learning by memorization) fails to produce students who possess "the kind of higher-order thinking and problem-solving abilities" they will need to compete and get along in this century. Specifically, their findings call for early childhood education that includes "active, hands-on, cooperative learning and interactive teaching" that "exposes children to meaningful, relevant learning experiences."

FACT: The Perry Project, a long-term study of early education, shows that children who received *high-quality* early education are more likely to finish high school, go on to college, earn more money, and stay away from drugs and crime.

Not all early childhood education facilities are created equally. An inferior program will not produce the spectacular results you want for your child in the vital early years.

Yes, children enrolled in quality programs get a jump start. And no, not any old program will do. With images of clean, safe, loving environments dancing in a parent's head—environments where children are intellectually stimulated, emotionally cared for, and socially integrated—it's a disappointing reality that, too often, glorified babysitting programs and day care centers are passed off as early childhood education programs.

A quality early childhood education program is exactly what it sounds like: a nurturing, educational experience for young children.

The variables in the quality of early childhood education and care are many.

Below are the keys that The Visone Method has proven will unlock the door to a high-quality early childhood education. *All* of the keys combined make up the foundation for early learning and later academic success. *All* should be included in the early childhood education program you choose as a parent or are involved with as an educator.

Since The Visone Method requires that these skills work together synergistically, rather than emphasizing just one or two, as many early childhood education programs might, these fifteen keys are not listed in any particular order. Each is equally important.

1. SKILLS

A great early childhood education program will include the purposeful development of all of the following skills: social, emotional, motor, and cognitive (the ability to make judgments, reason, and think).

Each of these skills is necessary to round out a child's early education. They are dependent on each other: Social skills and physical dexterity influence cognitive development; cognitive skills play a big role in a child's social identity, as well as his motor competence.

Considering how critical all of these skills are, the following should be noticed when you are evaluating an early childhood education program or facility:

o Is there plentiful guided interaction between the children?

o How are disagreements between two or more children handled?

o If children are physically hurt, how does the staff comfort them?

o Are fine motor skills emphasized? Do the students participate in writing and art projects that develop these skills?

o   Are gross motor skills increased through physical activities such as jumping and tumbling? (The development of both fine and gross motor skills contribute to maximized learning.)

o   Is there a skills checklist by age? A variety of skills should be included. For example: How well can a four-year-old predict what will happen next in a story (cognitive skill), or draw a human figure with arms, legs, torso, and head (demonstrating motor as well as cognitive skills)? Teaching children these skills as a complete set during their early years goes a long way to ensuring they will be able to absorb a balanced education throughout their lifetime. Ask to see the school's written curriculum to assure you that all of these skills are being taught to your satisfaction. In addition, many regulating state agencies offer a list of skills that schools are required to teach (see Appendix).

2. PRIVATELY OWNED vs. FRANCHISE

In general, The Visone Method believes that there is an advantage to a privately owned and operated school versus one that is not. The advantage is in the important details that make up your child's daily life at school.

Everything—from concerns about a shy child making new friends, to decisions affecting the balance in the classroom, to how to present the school's image in the community—should be decided by owners who have personally assessed the situation and have ultimate authority.

A privately owned early childhood education program is like any other owner-operated business. When owners are on the premises full-time, tending personally to the daily operations and policies of the program to which you have entrusted your child, there is a much higher degree of attention to details.

When a teacher in the trenches every day is asked to follow a certain procedure by hands-on owners, the teacher can be confident that the directive is a result of firsthand knowledge. It will mirror that of the teacher's own experience.

With onsite owners, a teacher with a concern, or, for that matter, a parent with a concern, can go to the director and get the problem resolved immediately—as opposed to waiting days or more while attempts are made to reach an offsite owner for resolution. If the highest authority onsite is an employee with minimal decision-making power, problems cannot be addressed quickly. This concern should not be minimized: with schedules so tightly booked today, parents don't want to wait. And why should they, when it comes to their children?

As with most owner-operated businesses, an environment of professionalism prevails at an owner-operated school. This positive environment rubs off on the staff. Of course, the ultimate recipient of this professionalism is the child.

School owners who also teach in the classroom, or perform the duties of director, have a complete, concrete understanding of day-to-day classroom activities, events, and curriculum. They are also able to observe staff on a daily basis.

Frequently, private schools promote higher goals for staff as well as children. A privately owned school can set its own high standards, often above what a regulating agency requires. In a company-owned or franchised school, policies are set by corporate committees that are typically remote from the everyday business of working closely with the children.

The school you choose becomes the environment in which your child spends her time when she is not with you. Compared to an outside owner, onsite owners generally have a stronger passion for the school they oversee. This passion results in a healthy, positive relationship between the owners and teachers … and that relationship directly affects your child.

3. PHYSICAL SECURITY

The physical security of any school is, of course, of prime importance. The following are critical points concerning a child's safety:

o   Does the school have a written policy encompassing the full-time safety of the students that is strictly adhered to?

o   Is access to classrooms regulated and strictly enforced by the teachers and other staff? What are the sign-in and sign-out policies?

o   What safety net has been set up so a child won't go home with someone the parents have not approved? Does the school have emergency numbers on file for each child, as well as information on who is allowed to take the child home? Parents should be allowed to specify exactly who should and shouldn't be allowed to remove their child from the campus. These instructions should be followed to the letter.

o Are electrical outlets covered and is age-appropriate furniture plentiful?

o Is there a fire and emergency routine, and is it posted? Do both children and employees know the routine? Does the school have regular fire drills? Are telephone numbers for fire, police, and poison control posted? There must be a fire alarm system installed, and it should be in working order and good repair. A licensed facility is required to have smoke detectors, and fire extinguishers should be checked each year.

o Is there a freshly stocked first-aid kit? Is it kept under lock and key, along with medications and potentially dangerous cleaning chemicals? Are teachers aware of the location, and are they trained in the use of the first aid and fire fighting equipment? Are staff members trained in CPR?

o Is safety information regarding the playground equipment available or supplied upon request?

o Does the staff know where every child is at all times? Are children always supervised? The Visone Method calls for two teachers to be in the play area when children are there so that dangerous situations can be anticipated and avoided.

At HAFHA, a written safety policy is firmly mandated and enforced. For instance, teachers are instructed to check their classrooms for child-proofing *each day*. "Look at your classroom from a child's perspective," the manual dictates. Adult scissors and hot beverages are not to be left where a small child can reach them.

When an extensive safety protocol is in place, the early childhood education facility you are considering deserves high marks.

4. CLEANLINESS OF FACILITY

Cleanliness and good health go hand in hand. This is particularly true when it comes to very young children whose immune systems haven't yet been completely developed.

Cleanliness and optimal health standards should be a top priority in any early childhood education facility. It's another way the staff shows their pride in their work and workplace.

Cleanliness policies should be clearly stated in the teacher's manual. In addition, governing agencies have specific regulations about the appropriate way to clean tables, counters, changing tables, cots, toys, and, of course, caregivers' and children's hands. Those policies should also be available to you in writing.

The manual we provide to our teachers at HAFHA states what needs to be cleaned (and, specifically, how) on a daily and weekly basis.

Look for these clues to assess the level of cleanliness practiced at an early childhood education facility:

o   Are cots and cribs labeled with the names of the children who use them?

o   Are cots not allowed to be shared on the same day? When a child leaves or gives up the cot, it should be completely sanitized.

o   Are toys disinfected daily?

o   Are toys that are mouthed by a child removed and put aside until they can be disinfected?

o   Are tables disinfected rather than merely wiped down?

o   Are floors vacuumed and swept a minimum of once a day?

o   Do staff members wear gloves when diapering a child?

o   Does the school teach good cleanliness habits to their students as part of their curriculum? Children need to learn good hygiene habits to attend to their own personal care.

5. TEACHER CERTIFICATION

Many state agencies do not require child care centers to employ certified teachers. As a result, many staff members are low-wage, inexperienced child care providers. While they are most likely loving, nurturing people, they are not qualified to do more than babysit and play without purpose.

On the other hand, certified teachers give an early childhood education program the edge in academics and professionalism. For this, and other equally important reasons, The Visone Method recommends that the teaching staff at the early childhood education facility you choose be certified.

Do the teachers in the classroom hold a current certification? Is the certification relevant to the developmental programs they will be teaching?

As mentioned previously, there are several ways a teacher can be considered certified:

1. A four-year degree in early childhood education or a four-year degree in elementary education (the former would be preferable for a preschool teacher)

2. P–3 certification, covering preschool through third grade education

3. An associate's degree in early childhood education

4. Child Development Associate certification, with courses geared to ages zero through five

A school should go above and beyond the minimum governing agencies recommendations. This would mean, for instance, that the school has placed certified teachers in *every* classroom, as opposed to keeping only a few certified teachers on the payroll because they have to.

At HAFHA, non-certified child care workers are hired to lovingly care for infants and toddlers and are supervised by certified teachers in the same room.

Teachers in early childhood education classrooms should have, at minimum, an associate's degree in early childhood development. Teachers in the kindergarten and higher classrooms should have the same degree as required by the district's public schools: four years of early childhood study.

In addition to certification, teachers should be mandated by their employers to participate in trainings and obtain CEUs (Continuing Education Units) to keep current on information affecting early childhood development, elementary education, or a P–3 degree.

While not a government requirement, teachers in the early childhood education facility of your choice should also be certified in first aid and CPR.

6. STUDENT-TEACHER RATIO

Governing agencies in every state define the ratio of students per teacher (see Appendix). These must be maintained in order for an early childhood education facility to remain licensed.

Again, The Visone Method encourages searching for an early childhood education facility that exceeds the basic requirements. Doesn't it make sense? The more teachers in a classroom per child, the more individual attention a child will get.

Here are acceptable minimum ratios:

o **Infants:** one teacher for each four infants

o **Toddlers:** one teacher for six toddlers

o **Preschool (three-year-olds):** one teacher for each ten children

o **Pre-kindergarten (four-year-olds):** one teacher for each twelve students

o **Kindergarten (five-year-olds):** one teacher for each fifteen students

Keep in mind that these are minimums. At HAFHA, a kindergarten class has twenty-five students and two certified teachers.

7. SOPHISTICATION OF PROGRAMS AND CURRICULUM

A written curriculum defines the school's academic goals. How sophisticated the curriculum is depends on how the school views itself: primarily as babysitters, or as a place to teach while lovingly caring for the children in their charge.

While public schools continue to cut their budgets, decimating important programs and laying off wonderful teachers, good private schools continue to build their curricula toward a crescendo of excellence.

Science, the arts, physical education, and music are critical components of a child's early education. The following factors show how dedicated a school is to these programs:

o   Is the room set up to allow for these subjects?

o   Is there an area for art projects?

o   Are there art, music, science, and physical education teachers on the payroll—in *addition to* regular classroom teachers? If so, you can be more assured that these subjects will be taught in depth and by teachers specially trained.

o   Also, consider to what ages and how often these subjects are offered during the school week.

Choose a school that introduces science and the arts by age three and continues to emphasize these subjects throughout the upper grades. Inclusion of these subjects proves that the school understands that children learn at younger ages. With all the new research on how the young brain develops, a sophisticated curriculum will reflect this critically important understanding.

For instance, many public schools (and some old-thought private ones) still hold to the outdated belief that reading should not be taught until first grade. HAFHA integrates the latest research, which shows that kindergarten is where learning to read in earnest should start.

Another way to judge the sophistication of the curriculum is through testing. Does the school offer nationally recognized testing, such as TerraNova, to measure where students stand academically?

Location should no longer be a roadblock to a great education. Thanks to our high tech world, a school located in a small, rural community far from a cosmopolitan city center has the same access to information as their counterparts in midtown Manhattan, Los Angeles, or London.

Make it a point to investigate the school's curriculum in regard to technology. It is necessary for young children to be exposed to the latest technology so that they can be competitive in the world they are growing up in. No matter how you feel personally about technology, it is what the world of today's child is about.

The newest technology should also be utilized in the ways the school conducts their business. Do they have e-mail they check regularly so you can stay in touch? If the administration is not technologically savvy, how can the school set an example for their students? Children love to see how their learning is put to use in the real world.

A good early childhood education facility will also ensure that their teachers are involved in getting ongoing education; this is how staff remains at the top of their field. In each state, there is a governing agency that dictates how many hours of continuing education are required for certified public school teachers; your school should match and exceed that requirement for their own teachers. A school that values itself will keep its teachers informed because it is the best practice for all involved—especially for the children in their charge.

The director should personally monitor what happens in each classroom on a regular basis. This observation keeps teachers on target with the curriculum and set objectives.

A good private school will also have a thorough knowledge of the programs and curriculum taught in their local community schools.

At minimum, reviews of and revisions to the curriculum should occur yearly.

In large part, because of these policies and beliefs, The Visone Method continues to lead the way. The staff and owners inform themselves with the latest techniques and strategies for teaching today's young minds.

8. HEALTH POLICY AND PROCEDURES

Health policies and procedures should be clearly stated in writing. This is the only effective way for parents and staff to understand, follow, and teach the procedures.

Let's face it: kids come loaded with germs that can manifest into drippy noses, coughs, and more. No school can guarantee that your child will not pick up germs during the day; however, the school that adheres to a strict health policy has the highest success in containing communicable diseases and conditions such as colds, conjunctivitis ("pink eye"), and head lice. The best way to control germs is to follow and enforce good health practices.

A policy should be in place that spells out under what conditions a child will be sent home from school. Criteria should include acute diarrhea, sore throat, a temperature over 101 F, and skin rashes that last over twenty-four hours. A written policy helps parents determine if their child is well enough to be sent to school. The policy benefits not only the sick child, but also classmates who might otherwise be exposed.

This policy should also spell out under what conditions a sick child is ready to return to school, such as twenty-four hours after medication for conjunctivitis has begun.

These same standards should also pertain to staff.

Notices should be sent home if there is a possibility that the students have become exposed to a communicable disease or condition.

Under what circumstances, if any, will the school allow staff to dispense prescription medicine to a child? A Dispensing Medicine Form should be available that keeps track of the date, time, and quantity of medicine the child will be given. In addition, parents should fill out a permission slip and have a note from the child's doctor. Dosage information should be clearly stated on the medicine label.

Is there a nurse on the payroll who makes regular visits to the school or, better yet, has set hours onsite? Does the nurse regularly evaluate children's hearing, eyesight, and more?

Can you arrange for special services, such as speech therapy, through the school?

If your child is injured at school, you should be given a written accident report when you arrive to pick him up at the end of the day. (Naturally, if your child is seriously injured, you must be informed immediately.) An accident report should state what happened to the child and what care the child received. It should further state the time of the accident and whether there were any witnesses; which teachers were supervising the child; whether it was necessary to immediately notify a parent; and whether the child was dismissed from the school. The school should keep a copy of the accident report on file.

A good early childhood education facility will also inform parents about immunization requirements as dictated by state regulating agencies. A full health history on each child should be kept at the school.

You can also safely say that a school that ensures staff is trained in CPR and first aid, as well as employing a staff member with an EMT (emergency medical technician) certificate, demonstrates deep caring about the health of each child.

An Unusual Incident Form should be filled out in situations where a child may arrive at school with bruises or other indications of potential neglect or abuse.

Finally, cleanliness is, of course, an extremely important factor in maintaining optimal health.

9. EMERGENCY PROCEDURES

The perception about what "being safe" means has changed for our nation—indeed, for nations all over the world—since Sept. 11, 2001.

Raising young children in the uncertain world we live in means the early childhood education facility you choose must have carefully thought-out, written emergency procedures—procedures that are followed by all staff members—to provide peace of mind to the parents and a safety shield to the children.

To that end, a high-quality early childhood education facility will maintain up-to-date information on their young students at all times.

Some of the emergency policies should be spelled out:

o   There should be regularly documented, mandatory emergency drills. For example, a Fire Drill Log should state the time of the drill, how many teachers and students participated, weather conditions, and the duration of the drill.

o   How the staff is to respond in the event of a serious injury to a child should be standardized. For example, teachers should be instructed to keep their voices calm as they move the other children away from the area.

o   Locations of fire alarms and extinguishers should be clearly spelled out.

o   It should be spelled out under which circumstances either a parent or 911 should be notified first.

o   There should be a health policy and emergency procedure manual in each classroom.

Nothing helps parents feel more confident while away from their child than knowing he is protected and safe. Your early childhood education facility should recognize this fact and do what they can to protect children.

10. DISCIPLINE POLICY

There are many ways to discipline children. You will want to make sure that your early childhood education facility shares your perspective on acceptable discipline. Gentle, caring, positive reinforcement should be at the top of the list of discipline policies.

A high-quality early childhood education facility will post its discipline policy for all to read. Such a facility will also require that teachers learn how to carry out the discipline policies.

A teacher's top priority should be to talk to the child about unacceptable behavior, letting the child know that we all make mistakes. The child should always feel that he or she is loved, and the behavior is unacceptable, not the child.

Distraction and redirection are excellent discipline techniques. For example, the teacher might try giving the child a new project, changing the subject, or moving her to another area of the room. An explanation should accompany the redirection, explaining why the action was not acceptable: "You hurt your friend's feelings when you said he couldn't join your group."

If time out is used as a discipline tactic, the child should be told why he or she has been placed in a time out. This technique should not be practiced for more than a few minutes at a time. The common "rule" is one minute in time out for every year of life, up to seven minutes, though one to three minutes is plenty.

The use of a "time out chair" or other prop should be avoided, because it humiliates the child rather than teaches. Teachers and other adults should speak respectfully to the young child even as they are doling out discipline. Instead of specifying the child as being in time out, teachers should call it a chance to sit by herself to think about the behavior.

When the time out is over, the teacher and child should discuss a solution to the misbehavior (an apology, perhaps). The teacher should then accompany the child back into the active classroom so restitution can be made.

These gentle, guiding approaches, along with others with the same intent, suggest an environment where each child will learn appropriate behavior from trained adults truly interested in his or her ability to fit into society. This is the major goal of discipline.

If a particular child constantly acts out, a teacher should bring the situation to the attention of the director; in turn, the parents should be called in for a conference on how to handle the situation together.

11. FULLY LICENSED FACILITY

A license showing that the early childhood education facility is meeting current state criteria for certification should be prominently displayed. All state regulations should be strictly followed and violations, if any, taken care of immediately.

Department of Health regulators should visit the facility and award inspection certificates. These should include certification of water temperature in the bathrooms as well as in the kitchen. A certificate of occupancy stating that the building is safe and up to code should be displayed.

Current paperwork should be on file for each student, including the status of any current medical concerns. Background information on teachers, as well as the director, should be available for inspection.

Each state regulatory agency requires that specific documentation be completed and kept on file; parents previewing an early childhood education facility should make themselves aware of the relevant documents and the reasons they are required. Teachers should be fingerprinted, and their medical information and job references should be kept on file.

12. PARENTAL INVOLVEMENT

"The Two Sculptors"
by Helen C. McCormick

I dreamed I stood in a studio
and watched two sculptors there.
The clay they used was a young child's mind
and they fashioned it with care.
One was a teacher: the tools she used were
books and music and art.
The other, a parent, who worked with a
guiding hand and gentle, loving heart.
Day after day, the teacher toiled with
touch that was deft and sure
while the parent labored by her side
and polished and smoothed it o'er.
Each agreed one would have failed if one
had worked alone.
For behind the teacher stood the school
and behind the parent, the home.

An early childhood education facility should recognize that the parent is the child's first teacher. A solid relationship with parents must be established so that parents and teachers may form a partnership built on trust.

With fewer hours available for family time these days, an early childhood education facility should also help create opportunities for parents to interact with their children. Can parents volunteer in the classroom? Chaperone class trips?

An open door policy is a must: Parents should always have the right to visit the school at any time to observe activities, student-teacher relationships, or safety procedures. **Any school that discourages unannounced**

visits from parents should be dropped from your list of those being considered.

A great early childhood education facility will be happy to create and encourage parent-child and parent-child-teacher opportunities. At HAFHA, we sponsor a variety of these kinds of events. One of the favorites is "Mommy and Me" dates. Children practice what to say to Mommy on the date: "You look pretty today," or, "Thank you for spending the day with me." Then each small charge ushers their mommy to a restaurant, arm in arm, where songs, poems, and gifts are exchanged. One parent was so impressed by "Mommy and Me," she was moved to write HAFHA: "Preparing my son for that day," she wrote, "really taught him to understand the special relationship with his mother. We grew a much deeper bond. A week has gone by and he still tells me he loves me *several times* a day." Of course, there's a "Daddy and Me" version of this "date" as well.

Still another way HAFHA helps families have fun together is through community service projects and fundraising events. The school is widely recognized for producing an ever-growing list of charity events. These not only give back to the community, but teach the children it is better to give than receive. Firsthand knowledge of this principle will serve them for a lifetime, helping them to be good citizens.

Parents should be kept informed of activities they can be involved in through a variety of ways—including conferences, newsletters, and contact through the classroom parent. To assist parents, a full calendar of all scheduled events for the year should be provided so that parents can adjust their own busy calendars.

13. PARENT-TEACHER CONFERENCES

Parent-teacher conferences should be formally scheduled at least twice during the school year. The conference should be a positive meeting between the teacher and parents to discuss cooperative approaches to the child's academic, social, and emotional development.

These conferences are imperative because they allow the parents to understand their child's progress in school. In addition to how well their child recognizes letters and numbers, parents can learn if their child has been exhibiting a disability in speech or is showing overly aggressive tendencies.

One incident at HAFHA demonstrates how important parent-teacher conferences can be. An enthusiastic young girl loved to tell her teacher stories, but her speech was so garbled the teacher could not understand her. The teacher brought this to the parent's attention during the conference. At first, the parent was upset; after all, *she* understood her child's speech. As a direct result of this conference, however, the parent discovered that even her own family members could not understand the little girl, but were reluctant to tell her parents. The child got the attention she needed from a speech therapist and today speaks clearly. The conference brought the situation to light in a private and non-confrontational way.

During the conference, a portfolio of the child's work should be available for review, as well as a detailed written assessment of his development.

The report card should detail sub-headings under broader subject categories. For instance, HAFHA's kindergarten card reflects grades for nine categories under the general heading of Reading and Language Arts. Those include ratings in "Follows a sequence of directions," "Developing comprehension skills," and "Spelling."

The teacher should also be able to substantiate comments and grades with the child's tests and class projects.

In addition to formal conferences, parents want to feel that they can address emerging concerns. Parents should be able to talk to a teacher after the class day is done. If this is not possible for some reason, parents should be informed when and how they can make contact with teachers, as needed.

14. SCHEDULE

A schedule of age-appropriate activities, complete with times and days these activities occur, should be in writing so that parents are kept informed. A written schedule demonstrates that there is a planned curriculum, instead of endless hours of unguided free play without instruction.

Academics should not be the only curriculum that a child is exposed to during her hours at an early childhood education facility. Time should also be built into the schedule for free-choice indoor play activities, music and movement activities, outdoor play, and clean up.

The schedule should reflect both child-directed and teacher-directed activities and allow for flexibility. For instance, after a few days of inside play due to rain, a teacher should let children outside to burn off some energy when the sun finally comes out.

15. CONTRACTUAL AGREEMENTS

Contractual agreements between parents and the school must be clearly written and signed by the director and parent. Information pertaining to the school's discipline, health, and release policies must be included.

Prior to signing, parents should be fully versed in the terms and conditions of registration, including the following:

o   Is the contract annual or month-to-month?

o   What are the terms for withdrawing a student? (HAFHA requires thirty days notice.)

o   What are the exact financial obligations? (What are the tuition charges? When is tuition due? Are there late fees?)

o   What hours will the child be attending class?

o   What are drop-off and pick-up times, extended daycare hours, schedule alterations, and other schedule policies?

Of course, a parent must be given a signed copy of the agreement.

These fifteen key points are critical to the success of any early childhood education facility. Whether you are a parent or educator, it's vitally important that you look for evidence of *all* of these criteria to ensure the best possible start for the children in your care.

Chapter 21

The Visone Method—Lighting the Path to a New Era in Childhood Education

What makes The Visone Method so powerful? As we said in the beginning of this book, The Visone Method considers the whole child. The Visone Method combines proven philosophies about early childhood education with policies that ensure heartfelt nurturing. The children in our charge are treated with sensitivity, and we offer the same compassion to their families. We leave no stone unturned in our desire to prepare children for both academic and social achievement.

According to those closest to The Visone Method—its students and their parents—it has succeeded resoundingly.

> "Like most parents, my husband and I have high expectations. Your program has exceeded every single expectation we have."
>
> "Your work in the development of young children's minds does not go unnoticed. Every day that I drop off my little Ella at your school I know will be fantastic. Everyone makes us feel as if she is a star."
>
> "The wonderful care our precious Nicholas always receives gives us great peace of mind. Keep up the good work for all the fortunate children who come through your doors."
>
> "Robert was sometimes not very confident when he was the center of attention. With your encouragement, he is now comfortable to voice his opinions and speak in public."
>
> "The musicals and plays are such a nice gift to the parents."

"As a new working mom, I was anxious about leaving my daughter. You not only met her needs, but also helped her learn so many things. Thank you for not only making this a great year for her, but also for comforting me!"

"I have watched Alex grow from a crying toddler into an independent, mature little boy. It would not have been possible without the loving environment you offer."

"Our children will continue on as much better people as a result of your program."

The Visone Method proclaims that academics are but one component (albeit a vital component) of the new era in early childhood education. Exposing children to the best stage-by-stage developmental materials is just as important as academics are. Balancing music, drama, art, and motor-skill activities with high-level academic learning—all in a fun environment—is the key to a successful future for early childhood education.

A warm, supportive relationship between teacher and child; detailed policies that ensure a school is clean and safe; a program that focuses intently on the best resources, learning tools, and teaching techniques; the ongoing education of teachers—these are tools for success when children are cocooned in a nurturing learning environment.

As our children progress through a rapidly changing, technology-based era, The Visone Method reminds us that we cannot lose sight of basics. Yes, we must keep our little ones competitive using the tools of their generation, but we must not overlook their feelings and self-esteem. We must remember that each child is an individual who learns at his own pace and in his own style.

Whether you are a parent, teacher, child care provider, or someone who cares about children, we hope that reading this book has sharpened your understanding of how young children should be educated. Our intention has been to give everyone equal access to this remarkable Method, as well as important criteria to consider when making choices for the children in your life. In this way, all children, no matter where they live or what their circumstances, have the opportunity for an equal educational starting point.

Remember: the first years of a child's life make a permanent impact on the child's future. The roads we choose academically, socially, and emotionally as adults were paved in childhood.

Use The Visone Method to light that road for the children in your life.

Appendix: State Regulatory Agencies

Alabama   Department of Human Resources, www.dhr.state.al.us/

Alaska   Department of Health and Social Services, www.hss.state.ak.us

Arizona   Division of Children, Youth & Families (DCYF), www.azdes.gov/

Arkansas   Department of Health & Human Services, www.state.ar.us/dhs/homepage.html

California   Children & Family Services Division (CFSD), www.dss.cahwnet.gov/cdssweb/default.htm

Colorado   Family, Health & Wellness, www.cdhs.state.co.us/childWelfare

Connecticut   Department of Children & Families (DCF), www.state.ct.us/dcf/

Delaware   Department of Services for Children, Youth & Their Families (DSCYF), www.state.de.us/kids/

District of Columbia Child and Family Services Agency, www.cfsa.dc.gov/cfsa/site/default.asp

Florida   Department of Children & Families (DCF), www.state.fl.us/cf_web/

Georgia   Adolescent Health & Youth Development, www.dhr.state.ga.us/portal/site

Hawaii   Office of Youth Services (OYS), www.hawaii.gov/dhs/

Idaho   Department of Health & Welfare, www.healthandwelfare.idaho.gov/

Indiana   Department of Health & Welfare, www.state.in.us/fssa/

Illinois   Department of Children & Family Services (DCFS), www.state.il.us/dcfs/index.shtml

Iowa   Bureau of Family Health, www.dhs.state.ia.us/dhs2005/dhs_homepage/index.html

Kansas   Department of Social and Rehabilitation Services, www.srskansas.org/

Kentucky   Family Resources & Youth Services (FRYSC), http://chfs.ky.gov/

Louisiana   Child & Family Services, www.dss.state.la.us/

Maine   Office of Child & Family Services, www.maine.gov/dhhs/bcfs/index.htm

Maryland   Governor's Office for Children, www.dhr.state.md.us/

Massachusetts   Health & Human Services (HHS), www.mass.gov/

Michigan   Department of Human Services (DHS), www.michigan.gov/dhs

Minnesota   Minnesota Youth Program (MYP), www.dhs.state.mn.us/main/

Mississippi   Department of Human Services (DHS), www.mdhs.state.ms.us/

Missouri   Department of Human Services (DHS), www.dss.mo.gov/pr_cs.htm

Montana   Department of Public Health & Human Services (DPHHS), www.dphhs.mt.gov/index.shtml

Nebraska   Health & Human Services System (HHSS), www.hhs.state.ne.us/jus/jusindex.htm

Nevada	Division of Child & Family Services (DCFS), http://dcfs.state.nv.us/
New Hampshire	Department of Health & Human Services (DHHS), www.dhhs.state.nh.us/DHHS/DHHS_SITE/default.htm
New Jersey	Division of Youth & Family Services (DYFS), www.state.nj.us/dcf/index.shtml
New Mexico	Children, Youth & Families Department (CYFD), www.cyfd.org/
New York	Office of Youth Development (OYD), www.dfa.state.ny.us/
North Carolina	Youth & Family Services (YFS), www.ncdhhs.gov/
North Dakota	Department of Human Services, www.state.nd.us/humanservices/
Ohio	Ohio Department of Job & Family Services (ODJFS), http://jfs.ohio.gov/index.stm
Oklahoma	Department of Human Services, www.okdhs.org/
Oregon	Department of Human Services (DHS), www.oregon.gov/DHS/children/index.shtml
Pennsylvania	Pennsylvania Council of Children, Youth & Family Services (PCCYFS), www.dpw.state.pa.us/ServicesPrograms/ChildWelfare/
Rhode Island	Department of Children, Youth & Families (DCYF), www.dcyf.state.ri.us/
South Carolina	Department of Social Services (DSS), www.state.sc.us/dss/cps/index.html
South Dakota	Department of Social Services (DSS), http://dss.sd.gov/

Tennessee	Department of Children's Services (DCS), www.state.tn.us/youth/
Texas	Department of Family and Protective Services (DFPS), www.dfps.state.tx.us
Utah	Department for Child & Family Services (DCFS), www.dhs.state.ut.us/
Vermont	Department for Children & Families (DCF), www.dcf.state.vt.us/
Virginia	Bureau for Children & Families, www.dss.state.va.us/
Washington	Department of Social & Health Services (DSHS), www1.dshs.wa.gov/
West Virginia	Bureau for Children & Families, www.wvdhhr.org/bcf/
Wisconsin	Child/Youth Services, www.dhfs.state.wi.us/
Wyoming	Department of Family Services (DFS), http://dfsweb.state.wy.us/

CPSIA information can be obtained at www.ICGtesting.com
Printed in the USA
BVOW04s1854190813

329015BV00003B/200/P